COLLINS
TRAVEL
GEM

FRENCH

PHRASE BOOK

COLLINS
London and Glasgow

First published 1986

© William Collins Sons & Co Ltd 1986

latest reprint 1988

ISBN 0 00 459401-0

Consultant
Philippe Patry

Other Travel Gem
Phrase Books:

German

Italian

Spanish

Portuguese

Yugoslav

Greek

Printed in Great Britain

Your **Travel Gem** Phrase Book will prove an invaluable companion on your holiday or trip abroad. In a genuinely handy format, it gives you all you need to say for basic communication, with fast and direct alphabetical access to the relevant information. Be sure to pack it with your passport!

Its layout provides two means of quick alphabetical access:

> 99 practical topics arranged in A-to-Z order from ACCOMMODATION to WINTER SPORTS via such topics as MENUS, ROOM SERVICE and TAXIS. Each topic gives you the basic phrases you will need, and in many cases an additional list with useful extra words. Just flick through the pages to the topic you need to look up;

> an alphabetical index at the back - WORDS - listing up to 1400 key words found in the 99 topics, for fast access to words which do not immediately seem to belong to a particular topic (such as 'safety pin, lose, passport').

This way you have the possibility of browsing through topics, as in more traditional phrase books, as well as having the advantage of alphabetical listing. The best of both worlds.

For information on GRAMMAR, PRONUNCIATION, the ALPHABET or CONVERSION CHARTS, , just flick through the pages until you get to that topic in alphabetical order. Though **Travel Gems** do not assume prior knowledge of the foreign language, some basic facts about grammar will help you improvise and get more out of your conversations with local people.

Whenever relevant, travel information has been included. Some likely replies to what you might say have also been shown in several topics (such as DENTIST or DOCTOR).

Enjoy your stay!

There's been an accident Il y a eu un accident
eel ya oo ũnn aksee-dõn

I've crashed my car J'ai eu un accident avec ma voiture
zhay oo ũnn aksee-dõn avek ma vwatoor

Can I see your insurance certificate please? Est-ce que je peux voir votre carte d'assurance?
es kuh zhuh puh vwahr votr kart dasoo-rõns

We will have to report it to the police Il faut avertir la police
eel foh avehr-teer la polees

We should call the police Il faudrait appeler la police
eel fohdreh aplay la polees

He ran into me Il m'est rentré dedans
eel meh rõntray duhdõn

The brakes failed Les freins ont lâché
lay frãn õn lashay

He was driving too fast Il conduisait trop vite
eel kõndwee-zeh troh veet

He was too close Il était trop près
eel ayteh troh preh

He did not give way Il n'a pas laissé la priorité
eel na pa lessay la preeo-reetay

The car number was ... Le numéro de la voiture était ...
luh noomay-roh duh la vwatoor ayteh ...

He was coming from my right/left Il venait sur ma droite/gauche
eel vuhneh soor ma drwaht/gohsh

damage les dégâts *daygah*

documents les papiers *pa-pyay*

driving licence le permis de conduire *pehrmee duh kõndweer*

green card la carte verte *kart vehrt*

insurance company la compagnie d'assurances *kõnpa-nyee dasoo-rõns*

lawyer un avocat *avo-ka*

offence une infraction *ãnfrak-syõn*

police station le commissariat (de police) *komee-saree-a (duh polees)*

See also EMERGENCIES

Before you set off for a foreign country it is always advisable to obtain proper accident and medical insurance. Ambulances have to be paid for. There is no central number for you to dial, but each area has its own number which you will find displayed inside telephone boxes.

There has been an accident Il y a eu un accident
eel ya oo uñn aksee-doñ

Call an ambulance/a doctor Appelez une ambulance/un médecin
aplay oon oñboo-loñs/uñ maydsañ

He has hurt himself Il s'est fait mal
eel seh feh mal

I am hurt Je me suis fait mal
zhuh muh swee feh mal

He is seriously injured/bleeding Il est sérieusement blessé/Il saigne
eel eh say-ryuhz-moñ blessay/eel say-nyuh

He can't breathe/move Il ne peut pas respirer/bouger
eel nuh puh pa reh-spee-ray/boo-zhay

I can't move my arm/leg Je ne peux pas bouger le bras/la jambe
zhuh nuh puh pa boo-zhay luh brah/la zhoñb

Cover him up Couvrez-le
koovray-luh

Don't move him Ne le bougez pas
nuh luh boo-zhay pa

He has broken his arm/cut himself Il s'est cassé le bras/s'est coupé
eel seh kassay luh brah/seh koopay

I have had a fall Je suis tombé
zhuh swee toñbay

bandage
le pansement
poñsmoñ

bitten
mordu
mordoo

dead
mort
mor

dislocate, to
disloquer
deeslo-kay

hospital
un hôpital
opee-tal

serious
grave
grav

slip, to
glisser
gleessay

sprain
une entorse
oñtors

stung
piqué
peekay

sunburn
le coup de soleil
koo duh solay

sunstroke
une insolation
añso-la-syoñ

See also HOTEL DESK, ROOM SERVICE, SELF-CATERING

We're looking for a hotel/an apartment
Nous cherchons un hôtel/un appartement
noo shehrshoñ uññ ohtel/uññ apart-moñ

I want to reserve a single/double room
Je voudrais réserver une chambre pour une personne/deux personnes
zhuh voodray rayzehr-vay oon shoñbr poor oon pehr-son/duh pehr-son

Is there a restaurant/bar? Est-ce qu'il y a un restaurant/un bar?
es keel ya uñ resto-roñ/uñ bar

Do you have facilities for the disabled?
Est-ce qu'il y a des aménagements prévus pour les handicapés?
es keel ya dayz amay-nazh-moñ prayvoo poor lay oñdee-kapay

I want bed and breakfast/full board Je voudrais une chambre avec petit déjeuner/avec la pension complète
zhuh voodray oon shoñbr avek puhtee day-zhuh-nay/avek la poñ-syoñ koñplet

What is the daily rate? Quels sont vos prix par jour?
kel soñ voh pree par zhoor

I want to stay three nights/from ... till ...
Je désire rester trois nuits/du ... au ...
zhuh dayzeer restay trwah nwee/doo ... oh ...

We'll be arriving at .../very late Nous arriverons à .../très tard
nooz areev-roñ a .../treh tar

Shall I confirm by letter? C'est nécessaire de confirmer par lettre?
seh naysay-sehr duh koñfeer-may par letr

---

balcony
le balcon
balkoñ
bathroom
la salle de bains
sal duh bañ
double bed
le grand lit
groñ lee
evening meal
le dîner
deenay
half-board
la demi-pension
duhmee-poñ-syoñ
lift
un ascenseur
asoñ-sur
lunch
le déjeuner
day-zhuh-nay
single bed
le lit pour une personne
lee poor oon pehr-son
with bath
avec salle de bains
avek sal duh bañ
with shower
avec douche
avek doosh
youth hostel
une auberge de jeunesse
ohberzh duh zhuh-nes

Where do I check in for the flight to Milan? Où est-ce que je dois me présenter pour le vol en partance pour Milan?
oo es kuh zhuh dwah muh prayzōn-tay poor luh vol ōn partōns poor meelōn

I'd like an aisle/a window seat Je voudrais une place couloir/fenêtre
zhuh voodray oon plas koolwahr/fuhnetr

Will a meal be served on the plane? Est-ce qu'on nous sert un repas à bord?
es kōn noo sehr ūn ruhpa a bor

Where is the snack bar/duty-free shop? Où est la cafétéria/la boutique hors-taxe?
oo eh la kafay-tay-rya/la booteek or-taks

Where can I change some money? Où est-ce que je peux changer de l'argent?
oo es kuh zhuh puh shōn-zhay duh lar-zhōn

Where do I get the bus to town? Où est-ce que je prends le bus pour aller en ville?
oo es kuh zhuh prōn luh boos poor alay ōn veel

Where are the taxis/telephones? Où sont les taxis/téléphones?
oo sōn lay taxi/taylay-fon

I want to hire a car Je voudrais louer une voiture
zhuh voodray loo-ay oon vwatoor

I am being met Quelqu'un vient me chercher
kelkūn vyān muh shehrshay

airport
un aéroport
a-ehro-por

baggage reclaim
la réception des bagages
raysep-syōn day bagazh

check-in desk
l'enregistrement des bagages
ōnruh-zheestruh-mōn day bagazh

flight
le vol
vol

land, to
atterrir
atay-reer

lounge
la salle (d'embarquement)
sal (dōnbar-kuhmōn)

non-smoking
non-fumeur
nōn-foomur

passport control
le contrôle des passeports
kōntrohl day pas-por

plane
un avion
a-vyōn

The French alphabet is the same as the English one. The pronunciation of each letter is given below it in the following table, together with the word used conventionally for clarification when spelling something out.

A	comme	Anatole	N	comme	Nicolas
a	*kom*	*ana-tol*	*en*	*kom*	*neekoh-la*
B	for	**Berthe**	**O**	for	**Oscar**
bay		*behrt*	*oh*		*oskar*
C		**Célestin**	**P**		**Pierre**
say		*sayles-tãn*	*pay*		*pyehr*
D		**Désiré**	**Q**		**Quintal**
day		*dayzee-ray*	*koo*		*kãntal*
E		**Eugène**	**R**		**Raoul**
uh		*uh-zhen*	*ehr*		*ra-ool*
F		**François**	**S**		**Suzanne**
ef		*frõnswah*	*es*		*soozan*
G		**Gaston**	**T**		**Thérèse**
zhay		*gastõn*	*tay*		*tayrez*
H		**Henri**	**U**		**Ursule**
ash		*õnree*	*oo*		*oorsool*
I		**Irma**	**V**		**Victor**
ee		*eerma*	*vay*		*veektor*
J		**Joseph**	**W**		**William**
zhee		*zhohzef*	*doo-bluh-vay*		*weel-yam*
K		**Kléber**	**X**		**Xavier**
ka		*klaybehr*	*eex*		*za-vyay*
L		**Louis**	**Y**		**Yvonne**
el		*loo-ee*	*ee grek*		*eevon*
M		**Marcel**	**Z**		**Zoé**
em		*marsel*	*zed*		*zoh-ay*

Is it far/expensive? Est-ce que c'est loin/cher?
es kuh seh lwañ/shehr

Are you Mr. Dubois? Est-ce que vous êtes Monsieur Dubois?
es kuh vooz eht ...

Do you understand? Est-ce que vous comprenez?
es kuh voo kõñpruh-nay

Can I go in there? Est-ce que je peux y entrer?
es kuh zhuh puh ee õñtray

Can you help me? Est-ce que vous pouvez m'aider?
es kuh voo poovay meday

Where is the chemist's? Où est la pharmacie?
oo eh la farma-see

When will it be ready? Ça sera prêt quand?
sa suhra preh kõñ

How do I get there? Je peux y aller comment?
zhuh puh ee alay komõñ

How far is it to ...? A quelle distance est ...?
a kel deestõñs eh ...

Is there a good restaurant? Est-ce qu'il y a un bon restaurant?
es keel ya uñ bõñ resto-rõñ

What is this? Qu'est-ce que c'est, ça?
kes kuh seh sa

Which is your room? Quelle est votre chambre?
kel eh votr shõñbr

Who is coming? Qui vient?
kee vyañ

How much is it? C'est combien?
seh kõñ-byañ

How many kilometres? Combien de kilomètres?
kõñ-byañ duh keeloh-metr

Is this the bus for ...? Est-ce que ce bus va à ...?
es kuh suh boos va à ...

Is it possible to hire a car? Est-ce que c'est possible de louer
une voiture?
es kuh seh posee-bluh duh loo-ay oon vwatoor

Bathing conditions are indicated by the following flags: red = unsafe; orange = unsafe, but lifeguards present; green = safe.

Is it safe to swim here? Est-ce qu'on peut se baigner ici sans danger?
es koñ puh suh bay-nyay eesee soñ doñ-zhay

When is high/low tide? La mer est haute/basse quand?
la mehr eh oht/bas koñ

How deep is the water? Quelle est la profondeur de l'eau?
kel eh la profoñ-dur duh loh

Are there strong currents? Est-ce qu'il y a de forts courants?
es keel ya duh for kooroñ

Is it a private/quiet beach? Est-ce que c'est une plage privée/tranquille?
es kuh seh oon plazh preevay/troñkeel

Where do we change? Où est-ce qu'on se change?
oo es koñ suh shoñzh

Is it possible to hire a deck chair/boat? Est-ce qu'il est possible de louer une chaise longue/un bateau?
es keel eh poseebl duh loo-ay oon shez loñg/uñ batoh

Can I go fishing/windsurfing? Est-ce que je peux aller à la pêche/faire de la planche à voile?
es kuh zhuh puh alay a la pesh/fehr duh la ploñsh a vwahl

Is there a children's pool? Est-ce qu'il y a un petit bain pour les enfants?
es keel ya uñ puhtee bañ poor layz oñfoñ

armbands les flotteurs de natation
flotur duh nata-syoñ

bucket le seau
soh

lifeguard le surveillant de plage
soorvay-yoñ duh plazh

sea la mer
mehr

spade la pelle
pel

sunglasses les lunettes de soleil
loonet duh solay

sunshade le parasol
para-sol

suntan oil l'huile solaire
weel solehr

swimsuit le maillot de bain
mye-yoh duh bañ

towel la serviette
sehr-vyet

ankle	**face**	**mouth**
la cheville	le visage	la bouche
shuhveey	*veezazh*	*boosh*
arm	**finger**	**muscle**
le bras	le doigt	le muscle
bra	*dwah*	*mooskl*
back	**foot**	**neck**
le dos	le pied	le cou
doh	*pyay*	*koo*
body	**hand**	**nose**
le corps	la main	le nez
kor	*mãn*	*nay*
bone	**head**	**shoulder**
un os	la tête	une épaule
os	*tet*	*aypohl*
breast	**heart**	**skin**
le sein	le cœur	la peau
sãn	*kur*	*poh*
buttocks	**joint**	**stomach**
les fesses	une articulation	un estomac
fes	*artee-koola-syõn*	*esto-ma*
cheek	**kidney**	**throat**
la joue	le rein	la gorge
zhoo	*rãn*	*gorzh*
chest	**knee**	**thumb**
la poitrine	le genou	le pouce
pwahtreen	*zhuhnoo*	*poos*
ear	**leg**	**toe**
une oreille	la jambe	un orteil
oray	*zhõnb*	*ortay*
elbow	**liver**	**tongue**
le coude	le foie	la langue
kood	*fwah*	*lõng*
eye (eyes)	**lung**	**wrist**
un œil (les yeux)	le poumon	le poignet
uhy (yuh)	*poomõn*	*pwah-nyay*

See also CAR PARTS

My car has broken down Ma voiture est
en panne
ma vwatoor eh oñ pan

**There is something wrong with the
brakes** Il y a un problème de freins
eel ya uñ problem duh fräñ

I have run out of petrol Je suis en panne
d'essence
zhuh swee oñ pan dessoñs

**There is a leak in the petrol
tank/radiator** Il y a une fuite dans le
réservoir d'essence/dans le radiateur
*eel ya oon fweet doñ luh rayzehr-vwahr
dessoñs/doñ luh radya-tur*

The windscreen has shattered Le pare-
brise est cassé
luh parbreez eh kassay

The engine is overheating Le moteur
chauffe
luh motur shohf

Can you tow me to a garage? Pouvez-
vous me remorquer jusqu'à un garage?
*poovay-voo muh ruhmor-kay zhooska uñ
garazh*

**Can you send a mechanic/a breakdown
van?** Est-ce que vous pouvez envoyer
un mécanicien/une dépanneuse?
*es kuh voo poovay oñvwah-yay uñ
mayka-nee-syäñ/oon daypa-nuhz*

Do you have the parts? Avez-vous les
pièces de rechange?
avay-voo lay pyess duh ruhshoñzh

Can you do a temporary repair? Pouvez-
vous faire une réparation provisoire?
*poovay-voo fehr oon raypa-ra-syoñ
proveez-wahr*

bulb
une ampoule
oñpool

**emergency
windscreen**
le pare-brise de
secours
*parbreez duh
suhkoor*

flat tyre
la crevaison
kruhveh-zoñ

hazard lights
le signal de
détresse
*see-nyal duh
daytress*

jack
le cric
kreek

jump leads
les câbles de
raccordement de
batterie
*kabl duh rakord-
moñ duh batree*

spanner
la clé
klay

warning triangle
le triangle de
présignalisation
*tree-oñ-gluh duh
praysee-nyalee-za-
syoñ*

wheel brace
le vilebrequin
(démonte-roue)
*veelbruh-käñ
(daymoñt-roo)*

I have an appointment with Mr. Dubois J'ai un rendez-vous avec Monsieur Dubois
zhay uñ rōñday-voo avek ...

He is expecting me Il m'attend
eel matōñ

Can I leave a message with his secretary? Est-ce que je peux laisser un message a sa secrétaire?
es kuh zhuh puh lessay uñ messazh a sa suhkray-tehr

I am free tomorrow morning Je suis libre demain matin
zhuh swee leebr duhmañ matañ

Here is my business card Voici ma carte (de visite)
vwahsee ma kart (duh veezeet)

Can I send a telex from here? Est-ce que je peux envoyer un télex d'ici?
es kuh zhuh puh ōñvwah-yay uñ tayleks deesee

Where can I get some photocopying done? Où est-ce que je pourrais faire faire des photocopies?
oo es kuh zhuh pooray fehr fehr day fohtoh-kopee

I want to send this by courier Je voudrais envoyer cela par service de messagerie
zhuh voodray ōñvwah-yay suhla par sehrvees duh messa-zhree

I will send you further details/a sample Je vous enverrai de plus amples détails/un échantillon
zhuh vooz ōñveh-ray duh plooz ōñpl daytye /uñ ayshōñ-tee-yōñ

Have you a catalogue/some literature? Est-ce que vous avez un catalogue/des brochures?
es kuh vooz avay uñ kata-log /day broshoor

I am going to the trade fair/the exhibition Je vais à la foire commerciale/à l'exposition
zhuh veh a la fwahr komehr-syal /a lekspoh-zee-syōñ

See also COLOURS AND SHAPES, DESCRIBING THINGS,
   MEASUREMENTS AND QUANTITIES, PAYING, SHOPPING

Do you sell postcards/milk? Est-ce que
vous vendez des cartes postales/du lait?
*es kuh voo vōnday day kart pos-tal/doo
leh*

How much is that? Ça coûte combien?
sa koot kōn-byān

Have you anything smaller/bigger? Est-
ce que vous avez quelque chose de plus
petit/de plus grand?
*es kuh vooz avay kelkuh shohz duh ploo
puhtee/duh ploo grōn*

Have you got any bread/matches? Est-ce
que vous avez du pain/des allumettes?
*es kuh vooz avay doo pān/dayz aloo-
met*

I'd like a newspaper/some apples Je
voudrais un journal/des pommes
zhuh voodray ūn zhoornal/day pom

A packet of cigarettes please Un paquet
de cigarettes, s'il vous plaît
ūn pakay duh seega-ret seel voo pleh

I prefer this one Je préfère celui-ci
zhuh prayfehr suh-lwee-see

I'd like to see the one in the window Je
voudrais voir celui qui est en vitrine
*zhuh voodray vwahr suh-lwee kee eh ōn
veetreen*

I'll take this one/that one there Je prends
celui-ci/celui-là
zhuh prōn suh-lwee-see/suh-lwee-la

Could you wrap it up for me? Est-ce
que vous pouvez me l'envelopper?
es kuh voo poovay muh lōn-vlopay

a kilo of
un kilo de
ūn keeloh duh

cheaper
moins cher
mwān shehr

department
le rayon
ray-yōn

department store
le grand magasin
grōn maga-zān

expensive
cher
shehr

shop
le magasin
maga-zān

supermarket
le supermarché
soopehr-marshay

100 grammes of
cent grammes de
sōn gram duh

There are a great number of official camping sites, many with excellent facilities. If you can't find a site, the local *syndicat d'initiative* may be able to help.

We are looking for a campsite Nous cherchons un camping
noo shehrshoñ uñ koñping

Do you have any vacancies? Est-ce que vous avez encore de la place?
es kuh vooz avay oñkor duh la plas

How much is it per night? C'est combien pour une nuit?
seh koñ-byañ poor oon nwee

We want to stay one night/one week Nous désirons rester une nuit/semaine
noo dayzee-roñ restay oon nwee/suhmen

May we camp here? Est-ce que nous pouvons camper ici?
es kuh noo poovoñ koñpay eesee

Can we park our caravan here? Pouvons-nous garer notre caravane ici?
poovoñ-noo garay notr kara-van eesee

Is there a shop/restaurant on the site? Est-ce qu'il y a une boutique/un restaurant dans le camping?
es keel ya oon booteek/uñ resto-roñ doñ luh koñping

Where is the washroom/drinking water? Où se trouvent les toilettes?/Où se trouve le robinet d'eau potable?
oo suh troov lay twalet/oo suh troov luh robee-neh doh pota-bluh

What facilities do you have on the site? Quelles sont les installations à la disposition des campeurs?
kel soñ layz añsta-la-syoñ a la deespoh-zee-syoñ day koñpur

air-mattress
le matelas pneumatique
matla pnuhma-teek

camp-bed
le lit de camp
lee duh koñ

fly sheet
le double toit
doobluh twah

gas cylinder
la bouteille de gaz
bootay duh gaz

guy rope
la corde (de tente)
kord (duh toñt)

mallet
le maillet
mye-yay

sleeping bag
le sac de couchage
sak duh kooshazh

tent
la tente
toñt

tent peg
le piquet de tente
peekay duh toñt

tent pole
le montant de tente
moñtoñ duh toñt

trailer
la remorque
ruhmork

I want to hire a car Je voudrais louer une voiture
zhuh voodray loo-ay oon vwatoor

I need a car with a chauffeur J'ai besoin d'une voiture avec chauffeur
zhay buhzwañ doon vwatoor avek shohfur

I want a large/small car Je voudrais une grande/petite voiture
zhuh voodray oon groñd/puhteet vwatoor

Is there a charge per kilometre? Est-ce que le kilométrage est en plus?
es kuh luh keeloh-maytrazh eh oñ ploos

How much extra is the comprehensive insurance cover? Il y a un supplément de combien pour l'assurance tous-risques?
eel ya uñ sooplay-moñ duh koñ-byañ poor lasoo-roñs too-reesk

I would like to leave the car in Paris Je voudrais laisser la voiture à Paris
zhuh voodray lessay la vwatoor a paree

My husband/wife will be driving as well Mon mari/Ma femme conduira aussi
moñ maree/ma fam koñdwee-ra ohsee

Is there a radio? Est-ce qu'il y a une auto-radio?
es keel ya oon ohtoh-ra-dyo

How do I operate the controls? Comment fonctionnent les commandes?
komoñ foñksyon lay komoñd

Please explain the car documents Expliquez-moi les papiers de la voiture, s'il vous plaît
eksplee-kay-mwah lay pa-pyay duh la vwatoor seel voo pleh

accelerator
l'accélérateur
aksay-layra-tur

alternator
un alternateur
altehr-natur

automatic
la voiture
automatique
vwatoor ohtoh-mateek

battery
la batterie
batree

bonnet
le capot
kapoh

boot
le coffre
kofr

brake fluid
le liquide pour
freins
leekeed poor frãn

brakes
les freins
frãn

cable
le câble
kahbl

carburettor
le carburateur
karboo-ratur

choke
le starter
starter

clutch
l'embrayage
õnbray-yazh

distributor
le delco
delkoh

dynamo
la dynamo
deena-moh

engine
le moteur
motur

exhaust pipe
le pot
d'échappement
poh dayshap-mõn

fan belt
la courroie de
ventilateur
koorwah duh võntee-latur

fuse
le fusible
foozee-bluh

gears
les vitesses
veetess

handbrake
le frein à main
frãn a mãn

headlights
les phares
far

hose
la durit
dooreet

ignition
l'allumage
aloo-mazh

indicator
le clignotant
klee-nyotõn

points
les vis platinées
vees platee-nay

radiator
le radiateur
radya-tur

reversing lights
les phares de
recul
far duh ruhkool

shock absorber
un amortisseur
amor-teesur

spark plugs
les bougies
boo-zhee

steering
la direction
deerek-syõn

steering wheel
le volant
volõn

tyre
le pneu
pnuh

wheel
la roue
roo

windscreen
le pare-brise
parbreez

**windscreen
washer**
le lave-glace
lavglas

**windscreen
wiper**
un essuie-glace
eswee-glas

See also PUBLIC HOLIDAYS

When are the local festivals? Quelles sont les dates des festivités dans la région?
kel sōñ lay dat day festee-veetay dōñ la ray-zhyōñ

Happy birthday! Bon anniversaire!
bon anee-vehrsehr

Merry Christmas! Joyeux Noël!
zhwah-yuh no-el

Happy New Year! Bonne Année!
bon anay

Congratulations! Félicitations!
faylee-seeta-syōñ

Best wishes for ... Tous mes vœux pour...
too may vuh poor ...

Have a good time! Amusez-vous bien!
amoo-zay-voo byáñ

Cheers! A la vôtre! or Santé!
a la vohtr or *sōñtay*

Enjoy your meal! Bon appétit!
bon apay-tee

It's our anniversary C'est notre anniversaire de mariage
seh notr anee-vehrsehr duh ma-ryazh

at Christmas
à Noël
a no-el
baptism
le baptême
batem
birthday
un anniversaire
anee-vehrsehr
christening
le baptême
batem
holiday
les vacances
vakōñs
New Year
le Nouvel An
noovel ōñ
party
la soirée (entre amis)
swahray ōñtra-mee
public holiday
le jour férié
zhoor fayree-ay
wedding
le mariage
ma-ryazh

I want something for a headache/a sore throat Je voudrais quelque chose pour le mal de tête/le mal de gorge
zhuh voodray kelkuh shohz poor luh mal duh tet / luh mal duh gorzh

I would like some aspirin/sticking plaster Je voudrais de l'aspirine/du sparadrap
zhuh voodray duh laspee-reen / doo spara-dra

Have you anything for sunburn/insect bites/diarrhoea? Je voudrais quelque chose pour les coups de soleil/les piqûres d'insectes/la diarrhée
zhuh voodray kelkuh shohz poor lay koo duh solay / lay peekoor dãnsekt / la dee-aray

I have a cold/I have a cough Je suis enrhumé/Je tousse
zhuh swee õnroo-may / zhuh tooss

Is this suitable for hay fever/an upset stomach? C'est bon pour le rhume des foins/un dérangement gastrique?
seh bõn poor luh room day fwãn / ũn dayrõnzh-mõn gastreek

How much/How many do I take? J'en prends combien?
zhõn prõn kõn-byãn

How often do I take it? J'en prends tous les combien?
zhõn prõn too lay kõn-byãn

Is it safe for children? C'est sans danger pour les enfants?
seh sõn dõn-zhay poor layz õnfõn

How do I get reimbursed? Je me fais rembourser comment?
zhuh muh feh rõnboor-say komõn

antiseptic
un antiseptique
õntee-septeek

bandage
le pansement
põnsmõn

contraceptives
les contraceptifs
kõntra-septeef

cotton wool
le coton
kotõn

cream
la crème
krem

insect repellant
la crème anti-insecte
krem õntee-ãnsekt

laxative
le laxatif
laksa-teef

prescription
une ordonnance
ordo-nõns

sanitary towels
les serviettes hygiéniques
sehr-vyet ee-zhyay-neek

tampons
les tampons
tõnpõn

tissues
les mouchoirs en papier
mooshwahr õn pa-pyay

I have a small baby/two children J'ai un
petit bébé/2 enfants
zhay ũn puhtee baybay / duhz õnfõn

Do you have a special rate for children?
Y a-t-il une réduction pour les enfants?
*ee ateel oon raydook-syõn poor layz
õnfõn*

Do you have facilities for children?
Qu'est-ce qui est prévu pour les
enfants?
kes kee eh prayvoo poor layz õnfõn

Have you got a cot for the baby? Avez-
vous un petit lit pour le bébé?
avay-voo ũn puhtee lee poor luh baybay

Where can I feed the baby? Où est-ce
que je peux allaiter le bébé?
oo es kuh zhuh puh alay-tay luh baybay

Where can I warm the baby's bottle? Où
est-ce que je peux faire chauffer le
biberon du bébé?
*oo es kuh zhuh puh fehr shohfay luh
beebuh-rõn doo baybay*

Is there a playroom? Est-ce qu'il y a une
salle de jeux?
es keel ya oon sal duh zhuh

Is there a babysitting service? Est-ce
qu'il y a un service de babysitting?
*es keel ya ũn sehrvees duh baybee-
seeting*

My son is six and my daughter is nine
Mon fils a six ans et ma fille a neuf ans
*mõn fees a seez õn ay ma feey a nuhv
õn*

baby food
les petits pots
puhtee poh
babysitter
le/la babysitter
baybee-seetehr
boy
le garçon
garsõn
child
un enfant
õnfõn
disposable nappies
les couches à jeter
koosh a zhuhtay
dummy
la sucette
sooset
girl
la fille
feey
high chair
la chaise haute
shez oht
nappy
la couche
koosh
pram
la voiture d'enfant
vwatoor dõnfõn
push chair
la poussette
pooset

Where is the nearest church? Où est
l'église la plus proche?
oo eh laygleez la ploo prosh

Where is there a Protestant church? Où
est-ce qu'il y a une église protestante?
oo es keel ya oon aygleez protes-tõnt

I want to see a priest Je voudrais voir un
prêtre
zhuh voodray vwahr ũn pretr

What time is the service (religieux)? A quelle heure
est le service (religieux)?
a kel ur eh luh sehrvees (ruhlee-zhee-uh)

I want to go to confession Je voudrais
aller me confesser
zhuh voodray alay muh kõn-fessay

altar
un autel
ohtel
candle
la bougie
boo-zhee
cathedral
la cathédrale
katay-dral
Catholic
catholique
kato-leek
chapel
la chapelle
shapel
churchyard
le cimetière
seem-tyehr
mass
la messe
mes
minister
le pasteur
pastur
mosque
la mosquée
moskay
rabbi
le rabbin
rabãn
synagogue
la synagogue
seena-gog

Does this bus/train go to ...? Est-ce que ce bus/train va à ...?
es kuh suh boos/trañ va a ...

Where do I get a bus for the airport/cathedral? Où est-ce que je prends le bus pour aller à l'aéroport/à la cathédrale?
oo es kuh zhuh prõn luh boos poor alay a la-ehro-por/a la katay-dral

Which bus do I take for the museum? Quel bus va au musée?
kel boos va oh moozay

Where do I change/get off? Où est-ce que je change/descends?
oo es kuh zhuh shõnzh/dessõ

How frequent are the buses/trains to the city centre? Il y a des bus/trains pour le centre-ville tous les combien?
eel ya day boos/trañ poor luh sõntr-veel too lay kõñ-byañ

Where is the nearest underground station? Où est la station de métro la plus proche?
oo eh la sta-syõñ duh maytroh la ploo prosh

What is the fare to the town centre? Ça coûte combien pour aller au centre-ville?
sa koot kõñ-byañ poor alay oh sõntr-veel

Where do I buy a ticket? Où est-ce qu'on achète un ticket?
oo es kõñ a-shet uñ teekeh

What time is the last bus? A quelle heure est le dernier bus?
a kel ur eh luh dehr-nyay boos

book of tickets le carnet de tickets
karneh duh teekeh

bus stop un arrêt
areh

conductor le receveur
ruhsuh-vur

driver le conducteur
kõñdook-tur

escalator un escalier roulant
eska-lyay roolõñ

half fare le demi-tarif
duhmee-tareef

lift un ascenseur
asõñ-sur

season ticket un abonnement
abon-mõñ

tourist ticket le billet touristique
bee-yay toorees-teek

underground le métro
maytroh

A dry cleaner's (*une teinturerie: tãñtoo-ruhree* or *un pressing: pressing*) is sometimes combined with a laundry (*une blanchisserie: blõñshee-suhree*). A launderette is *une laverie automatique: lavree ohtoh-mateek.*

Is there a laundry service? Y a-t-il un service de blanchissage?
ee ateel uñ sehrvees duh blõñshee-sazh

Is there a launderette/dry cleaner's nearby? Est-ce qu'il y a une laverie automatique/un pressing près d'ici?
es keel ya oon lavree ohtoh-mateek / uñ presseeng preh deesee

Where can I get this skirt cleaned/ironed? Où est-ce que je peux faire nettoyer/faire repasser cette jupe?
oo es kuh zhuh puh fehr netwah-yay / fehr ruh-passay set zhoop

Where can I do some washing? Où est-ce que je peux faire un peu de lessive?
oo es kuh zhuh puh fehr uñ puh duh lesseev

I need some soap and water J'ai besoin de savon et d'un peu d'eau
zhay buhzwãñ duh savõñ ay duñ puh doh

Can you remove this stain? Est-ce que vous pouvez faire partir cette tache?
es kuh voo poovay fehr parteer set tash

This fabric is very delicate C'est un tissu très délicat
seh uñ teesoo treh daylee-ka

When will my things be ready? Mes affaires seront prêtes quand?
mayz afehr suhrõñ pret kõñ

clothes	les vêtements
	vetmõñ
disinfectant	le désinfectant
	dayzãñ-fektõñ
dry, to	sécher
	sayshay
sink	un évier
	ay-vyay
tap	le robinet
	robee-neh
wash, to	laver
	lavay
washbasin	le lavabo
	lava-boh
washing powder	la lessive
	lesseev

I take a continental size 40 Je prends du 40
zhuh prõn doo karõnt

Can you measure me? Est-ce que vous pouvez prendre mes mesures?
es kuh voo poovay prõndr may muhzoor

May I try on this dress? Est-ce que je peux essayer cette robe?
es kuh zhuh puh essay-yay set rob

May I take it over to the light? Est-ce que je peux la voir à la lumière?
es kuh zhuh puh la vwahr a la loo-myehr

Where are the changing rooms? Où sont les cabines d'essayage?
oo sõn lay kabeen dessay-yazh

Is there a mirror? Est-ce que vous avez une glace?
es kuh vooz avay oon glas

It's too big/small C'est trop grand/petit
seh troh grõn/puhtee

What is the material? C'est fait en quoi?
seh feh õn kwa

Is it washable? Est-ce que c'est lavable?
es kuh seh lava-bluh

I don't like it Je ne l'aime pas
zhuh nuh lem pa

I don't like the colour Je n'aime pas la couleur
zhuh nem pa la koolur

belt
la ceinture
sãntoor

blouse
le chemisier
shuhmee-zyay

bra
le soutien-gorge
soo-tyãn-gorzh

button
le bouton
bootõn

cardigan
le gilet (de laine)
zheeleh (duh len)

clothes
les vêtements
vetmõn

coat
le manteau
mõntoh

cotton
le coton
kotõn

denim
la toile de jean
twal duh jeen

dress
la robe
rob

fabric
le tissu
teesoo

fur
la fourrure
fooroor

cont.

gloves
les gants
gõn

hat
le chapeau
shapoh

jacket
la veste
vest

jeans
le jean
jeen

lace
la dentelle
dõntel

leather
le cuir
kweer

nightdress
la chemise de nuit
shuhmeez duh nwee

nylon
le nylon
neelõn

pants
le slip
sleep

petticoat
le jupon
zhoopõn

polyester
le polyester
polee-estehr

pyjamas
le pyjama
pee-zhama

raincoat
un imperméable
ãnpehr-may-abl

sandals
les sandales
sõndal

scarf
une écharpe
aysharp

shirt
la chemise
shuhmeez

shoes
les chaussures
shohsoor

shorts
le short
short

silk
la soie
swah

skirt
la jupe
zhoop

socks
les chaussettes
shohset

stockings
les bas
ba

suede
le daim
dãn

suit (man's)
le costume
kostoom

suit (woman's)
le tailleur
tye-yur

sweater
le pull
pool

swimsuit
le maillot de bain
mye-yoh duh bãn

t-shirt
le T-shirt
tee-shurt

tie
la cravate
kravat

tights
le collant
kolõn

trousers
le pantalon
põnta-lõn

trunks
le slip (de bain)
sleep (duh bãn)

vest
le maillot de
corps
mye-yoh duh kor

wool
la laine
len

zip
la fermeture
éclair
*fehrm-toor
ayklehr*

Is there a bus to ...? Est-ce qu'il y a un bus pour ...?
es keel ya un boos poor ...

Which bus goes to ...? Quel bus va à ...?
kel boos va a ...

Where do I catch the bus for ...? Où est-ce que je prends le bus pour ...?
oo es kuh zhuh pron luh boos poor ...

What are the times of the buses to ...? Quel est l'horaire des bus pour ...?
kel eh lorehr day boos poor ...

Does this bus go to ...? Est-ce que ce bus va à ...?
es kuh suh boos va a ...

Where do I get off? Où est-ce que je descends?
oo es kuh zhuh desson

Is there a toilet on board? Est-ce qu'il y a des toilettes à bord?
es keel ya day twalet a bor

What time does it leave? Il part à quelle heure?
eel par a kel ur

What time does it arrive? Il arrive à quelle heure?
eel areev a kel ur

Will you tell me where to get off? Est-ce que vous pouvez me dire quand je dois descendre?
es kuh voo poovay muh deer kon zhuh dwah dessondr

Let me off here please Je voudrais descendre ici, s'il vous plaît
zhuh voodray dessondr eesee seel voo pleh

bus depot
la gare routière
gar roo-tyehr

driver
le conducteur
kondook-tur

film show
le film
feelm

luggage hold
le coffre
kofr

luggage rack
le porte-bagages
port-bagazh

seat
la place
plas

beige
beige
bayzh

big
grand
grõn

black
noir
nwahr

blue
bleu
bluh

brown
marron
marõn

circular
circulaire
seerkoo-lehr

crimson
pourpre
poorpr

cube
le cube
koob

dark
foncé
fõnsay

fat
gros
groh

flat
plat
plah

gold
doré
doray

green
vert
vehr

grey
gris
gree

lemon
citron
seetrõn

light
clair
klehr

long
long
lõn

mauve
mauve
mohv

oblong
rectangulaire
rektõn-goolehr

orange
orange
orõnzh

oval
ovale
oval

pink
rose
rohz

pointed
pointu
pwãntoo

purple
violet
vee-olay

red
rouge
roozh

round
rond
rõh

shade
le ton
tõn

shiny
brillant
bree-yõn

silver
argenté
ar-zhõntay

small
petit
puhtee

square
carré
karay

thick
épais
aypeh

thin
mince
mãns

turquoise
turquoise
toorkwahz

white
blanc
blõn

yellow
jaune
zhohn

This does not work Ça ne marche pas
sa nuh marsh pa

I can't turn the heating off/on Je ne peux pas fermer/ouvrir le chauffage
zhuh nuh puh pa fehrmay/oovrer luh shohfazh

The lock is broken La serrure est cassée
la sehroor eh kassay

I can't open the window Je ne peux pas ouvrir la fenêtre
zhuh nuh puh pa oovrer la fuhnetr

The toilet won't flush La chasse d'eau ne marche pas
la shas doh nuh marsh pa

There is no hot water/toilet paper Il n'y a pas d'eau chaude/de papier hygiénique
eel nya pa doh shohd/duh pa-pyay ee-zhyay-neek

The washbasin is dirty Le lavabo est sale
luh lava-boh eh sal

The room is noisy La chambre est bruyante
la shoñbr eh brwee-yoñt

My coffee is cold Mon café est froid
moñ kafay eh frwah

We are still waiting to be served On ne nous a pas encore servis
oñ nuh nooz a pa oñkor sehrvee

I bought this here yesterday J'ai acheté ça ici hier
zhay ashtay sa eesee yehr

It has a flaw/hole in it Il y a un défaut/un trou
eel ya uñ dayfoh/uñ troo

Hello/Goodbye Bonjour/Au revoir
bōñ-zhoor / oh ruhvwahr

How do you do? Comment allez-vous?
komōñt alay-voo

Do you speak English? Est-ce que vous parlez anglais?
es kuh voo parlay ōñgleh

I don't speak French Je ne parle pas français
zhuh nuh parl pa frōñseh

What's your name? Quel est votre nom?
kel eh votr nōñ

My name is ... Je m'appelle ...
zhuh mapel ...

Do you mind if I sit here? Ça ne vous dérange pas si je
m'assieds ici?
sa nuh voo dayrōñzh pa see zhuh ma-syay eesee

I'm English/Scottish/Welsh/Irish/American Je suis
anglais/écossais/gallois/irlandais/américain
zhuh swee ōñgleh / ayko-seh / galwah / eerlōñ-deh / amay-reekāñ

Are you French? Est-ce que vous êtes français?
es kuh vooz eht frōñseh

Would you like to come out with me? Est-ce que vous voulez
sortir avec moi?
es kuh voo voolay sorteer avek mwah

Yes, I should like to Oui, avec plaisir
wee avek playzeer

No, thank you Non, merci
nōñ mehrsee

Can you give me your address? Est-ce que vous pouvez me
donner votre adresse?
es kuh voo poovay muh donay votr a-dress

Yes please/No thank you Oui merci/Non merci
wee mehrsee / nõn mehrsee

Thank you (very much) Merci (beaucoup)
mehrsee (bohkoo)

I'm sorry Pardon
pardõn

I'm on holiday here Je suis en vacances ici
zhuh swee õn vakõns eesee

This is my first trip to Paris C'est la première fois que je viens
à Paris
seh la pruh-myehr fwa kuh zhuh vyãn a paree

Do you mind if I smoke? Ça ne vous dérange pas si je fume?
sa nuh voo dayrõnzh pa see zhuh foom

Would you like a drink? Est-ce que je peux vous offrir quelque
chose à boire?
es kuh zhuh puh vooz ofreer kelkuh shohz a bwahr

Have you ever been to Britain? Est-ce que vous êtes déjà allé
en Grande-Bretagne?
es kuh vooz et day-zha alay õn grõnd-bruhta-nyuh

Did you like it there? Est-ce que ça vous a plu?
es kuh sa vooz a ploo

What part of France are you from? D'où est-ce que vous venez
en France?
doo es kuh voo vuhnay õn frõns

In the weight and length charts, the middle figure can be either metric or imperial. Thus 3.3 feet=1 metre, 1 foot=0.3 metres, and so on.

feet		metres	inches		cm	lbs		kg
3.3	1	0.3	0.39	1	2.54	2.2	1	0.45
6.6	2	0.61	0.79	2	5.08	4.4	2	0.91
9.9	3	0.91	1.18	3	7.62	6.6	3	1.4
13.1	4	1.22	1.57	4	10.6	8.8	4	1.8
16.4	5	1.52	1.97	5	12.7	11	5	2.2
19.7	6	1.83	2.36	6	15.2	13.2	6	2.7
23	7	2.13	2.76	7	17.8	15.4	7	3.2
26.2	8	2.44	3.15	8	20.3	17.6	8	3.6
29.5	9	2.74	3.54	9	22.9	19.8	9	4.1
32.9	10	3.05	3.9	10	25.4	22	10	4.5
			4.3	11	27.9			
			4.7	12	30.1			

°C	0	5	10	15	17	20	22	24	26	28	30	35	37	38	40	50	100
°F	32	41	50	59	63	68	72	75	79	82	86	95	98.4	100	104	122	212

Km	10	20	30	40	50	60	70	80	90	100	110	120
Miles	6.2	12.4	18.6	24.9	31	37.3	43.5	49.7	56	62	68.3	74.6

Tyre pressures

lb/sq in	15	18	20	22	24	26	28	30	33	35
kg/sq cm	1.1	1.3	1.4	1.5	1.7	1.8	2	2.1	2.3	2.5

Liquids

gallons	1.1	2.2	3.3	4.4	5.5	pints	0.44	0.88	1.76
litres	5	10	15	20	25	litres	0.25	0.5	1

I have nothing to declare Je n'ai rien à déclarer
zhuh nay ryañ a daykla-ray

I have the usual allowances of alcohol/tobacco Je n'ai plus que
la quantité d'alcool/de tabac tolérée
zhuh nay ploo kuh la koñtee-tay dalkol/duh taba tolay-ray

I have two bottles of wine/a bottle of spirits to declare J'ai deux
bouteilles de vin/une bouteille d'alcool à déclarer
zhay duh bootay duh vañ/oon bootay dalkol a daykla-ray

My wife/husband and I have a joint passport Ma femme/Mon
mari et moi sommes sur le même passeport
ma fam/moñ maree ay mwah som soor luh mem paspor

The children are on this passport Les enfants sont sur ce
passeport
layz oñfoñ soñ soor suh paspor

I am a British national Je suis de nationalité britannique
zhuh swee duh na-syo-nalee-tay breeta-neek

I shall be staying in France for three weeks Je reste 3 semaines
en France
zhuh rest trwah suhmen oñ froñs

We are here on holiday Nous sommes ici en vacances
noo som eesee oñ vakoñs

I am here on business Je suis ici en voyage d'affaires
zhuh swee eesee oñ vwah-yazh dafehr

I have an entry visa J'ai un visa
zhay uñ veeza

See also NUMBERS

What is the date today?	Quelle est la date aujourd'hui?
	kel eh la dat oh-zhoordwee
It's the ...	C'est le ... *seh luh ...*

1st of March	**2nd of June**
premier mars	deux juin
pruh-myay mars	*duh zhwān*

We will arrive on the 29th of August Nous arriverons le
vingt-neuf août *nooz aree-vuhrōn luh vānt-nuhf oot*

1984 dix-neuf cent quatre-vingt-quatre *deez-nuhf-sōn katr-vān-katr*

Monday	lundi	*lūndee*
Tuesday	mardi	*mardee*
Wednesday	mercredi	*mehrkruh-dee*
Thursday	jeudi	*zhuhdee*
Friday	vendredi	*vōndruh-dee*
Saturday	samedi	*samdee*
Sunday	dimanche	*deemōnsh*

January	**May**	**September**
janvier	mai	septembre
zhōnvee-ay	*may*	*septōnbr*
February	**June**	**October**
février	juin	octobre
fayvree-ay	*zhwān*	*oktobr*
March	**July**	**November**
mars	juillet	novembre
mars	*zhwee-yeh*	*novōnbr*
April	**August**	**December**
avril	août	décembre
avreel	*oot*	*daysōnbr*

I need to see the dentist (urgently) Je dois voir le dentiste (d'urgence)
zhuh dwah vwahr luh dõnteest (door-zhõns)

I have toothache J'ai mal aux dents
zhay mal oh dõn

I've broken a tooth J'ai une dent de cassée
zhay oon dõn duh kassay

A filling has come out Un plombage est parti
ũn plõnbazh eh partee

My gums are bleeding/are sore Mes gencives saignent/me font mal
may zhõnseev say-nyuh/muh fõn mal

Please give me an injection Vous voulez bien me faire une piqûre
voo voolay byãn muh fehr oon peekoor

My dentures need repairing C'est nécessaire de réparer mon dentier
seh naysay-sehr duh raypa-ray mõn dõn-tyay

THE DENTIST MAY SAY:

Je dois l'enlever
zhuh dwah lõnluh-vay
I shall have to take it out

Il faut faire un plombage
eel foh fehr ũn plõnbazh
You need a filling

Ça va peut-être vous faire un peu mal
sa va puht-etr voo fehr ũn puh mal
This might hurt a bit

bad	hard	rough
mauvais	dur	rugueux
moveh	*door*	*rooguh*
beautiful	**heavy**	**short**
beau	lourd	court
boh	*loor*	*koor*
bitter	**horrible**	**slow**
amer	horrible	lent
amehr	*oree-bl*	*lōn*
clean	**hot**	**smooth**
propre	(très) chaud	lisse
propr	*(treh) shoh*	*lees*
cold	**interesting**	**soft**
froid	intéressant	doux
frwah	*āntay-resōn*	*doo*
difficult	**light**	**sour**
difficile	léger	acide
deefee-seel	*lay-zhay*	*aseed*
dirty	**long**	**spicy**
sale	long	épicé
sal	*lōn*	*aypee-say*
easy	**lovely**	**strong**
facile	charmant	fort
faseel	*sharmōn*	*for*
excellent	**near**	**sweet**
excellent	près	sucré
ekseh-lōn	*preh*	*sookray*
far	**new**	**unpleasant**
loin	nouveau	désagréable
lwān	*noovoh*	*dayza-gray-abl*
fast	**old**	**warm**
rapide	vieux	chaud
rapeed	*vyuh*	*shoh*
good	**pleasant**	**weak**
bon	agréable	faible
bōn	*agray-abl*	*febl*

Where is the nearest post office? La
  poste la plus proche, s'il vous plaît?
  la post la ploo prosh seel voo pleh

How do I get to the airport? Pour aller à
  l'aéroport, s'il vous plaît?
  poor alay a la-ehro-por seel voo pleh

Can you tell me the way to the station?
  Pour aller à la gare, s'il vous plaît?
  poor alay a la gar seel voo pleh

Is this the right way to the cathedral?
  Est-ce que c'est la direction de la
  cathédrale?
  es kuh seh la deerek-syõn duh la katay-
  dral

**I am looking for the tourist information
  office** Je cherche le syndicat d'initiative
  zhuh shersh luh sãndee-ka deenee-sya-
  teev

Is it far to walk/by car? Est-ce que c'est
  loin à pied/en voiture?
  es kuh seh lwãn a pyay /õn vwatoor

Which road do I take for ...? La route
  pour aller à ..., s'il vous plaît?
  la root poor alay a ... seel voo pleh

Is this the turning for ...? Est-ce que
  c'est là que je tourne pour ...?
  es kuh seh la kuh zhuh toorn poor ...

How do I get on to the motorway? Pour
  rejoindre l'autoroute, s'il vous plaît?
  poor ruh-zhwãndruh lohtoh-root seel voo
  pleh

Can you show me on the map? Est-ce
  que vous pouvez me montrer sur la
  carte?
  es kuh voo poovay muh mõntray soor la
  kart

corner
le coin
kwãn
left
à gauche
a gohsh
over
sur
soor
over there
là-bas
la-bah
right
à droite
a drwaht
road sign
le panneau de
signalisation
panoh duh see-
nyalee-za-syõn
straight on
tout droit
too drwah
through
à travers
a travehr
under
sous
soo

See also BODY, ACCIDENTS - INJURIES, DENTIST

Medical treatment has to be paid for on the spot. While form E111 (which should be obtained before departure) enables British and Irish visitors to reclaim a proportion of the costs, proper accident/medical insurance is still advisable.

I need a doctor J'ai besoin d'un docteur *zhay buhzwañ dūñ doktur*	**cough** la toux *too*
Can I make an appointment? Est-ce que je peux prendre rendez-vous? *es kuh zhuh puh proñdr roñday-voo*	**cut** la coupure *koopoor*
My wife is ill Ma femme est malade *ma fam eh malad*	**faint, to** s'évanouir *sayva-nweer*
I have a sore throat J'ai mal à la gorge *zhay mal a la gorzh*	**food poisoning** l'intoxication alimentaire *añtok-seeka-syoñ alee-moñtehr*
He has diarrhoea/earache Il a la diarrhée/Il a mal à l'oreille *eel a la dee-aray/eel a mal a loray*	**hay fever** le rhume des foins *room day fwañ*
I am constipated Je suis constipé *zhuh swee koñstee-pay*	**headache** le mal de tête *mal duh tet*
I have a pain here/in my chest J'ai mal ici/dans la poitrine *zhay mal eesee/doñ la pwahtreen*	**ill** malade *malad*
She has a temperature Elle a de la température *el a duh la toñpay-ratoor*	**inflamed** enflammé *oñfla-may*
He has been stung/bitten Il a été piqué/mordu *eel a aytay peekay/mordoo*	**injection** la piqûre *peekoor*
He can't breathe/walk Il a de la difficulté à respirer/marcher *eel a duh la deefee-kooltay a reh-spee-ray/marshay*	**medicine** le médicament *maydee-kamoñ*
I feel dizzy J'ai la tête qui tourne *zhay la tet kee toorn*	

I can't sleep/swallow J'ai de la difficulté à dormir/avaler
zhay duh la deefee-kooltay a dormeer/ava-lay

She has been sick Elle a vomi
el a vomee

I am a diabetic/pregnant Je suis diabétique/enceinte
zhuh swee dee-abay-teek/ōnsānt

I am allergic to penicillin/cortisone Je suis allergique à la pénicilline/à la cortisone
zhuh swee alehr-zheek a la paynee-seeleen/a la kortee-zon

I have high blood pressure Je fais de la tension
zhuh feh duh la tōn-syōn

My blood group is A positive/O negative Mon groupe sanguin est rhésus A positif/rhésus O négatif
mōn groop sōngān eh rayzoos a pozee-teef/rayzoos oh nayga-teef

THE DOCTOR MAY SAY:

Vous devez rester couché
voo duhvay restay kooshay
You must stay in bed

Il faut le transporter à l'hôpital
eel foh luh trōnspor-tay a lopee-tal
He will have to go to hospital

Il faut vous opérer
eel foh vooz opay-ray
You will need an operation

Prenez cela 3/4 fois par jour
pruhnay suhla trwah/katr fwah par zhoor
Take this three/four times a day

painful
douloureux
dooloo-ruh

pill
la pilule
peelool

poisoning
l'empoisonnement
ōnpwah-zonmōn

stomach upset
le dérangement gastrique
dayrōnzh-mōn gastreek

tablet
le comprimé
kōnpree-may

unconscious
sans connaissance
sōn koneh-sōns

DRINKS 36

See also WINES AND SPIRITS

A black/white coffee, please Un café noir/café crème, s'il vous plaît
uñ kafay nwahr/kafay krem seel voo pleh

Two cups of tea Deux thés
duh tay

A pot of tea Un pot de thé
uñ poh duh tay

A glass of lemonade Un verre de limonade
uñ vehr duh leemo-nad

A bottle of mineral water Une bouteille d'eau minérale
oon bootay doh meenay-ral

A draught beer Une bière à la pression
oon byehr a la preh-syoñ

With ice, please Avec des glaçons, s'il vous plaît
avek day glasoñ seel voo pleh

Do you have ...? Est-ce que vous avez ...?
es kuh vooz avay ...

Another coffee, please Encore un café, s'il vous plaît
oñkor uñ kafay seel voo pleh

beer
la bière
byehr
coke
le coca(-cola)
koka(-kola)
drinking chocolate
le chocolat chaud
shoko-la shoh
drinking water
l'eau potable
oh potabl
fruit juice
le jus de fruit
zhoo duh frwee
lemon tea
le thé au citron
tay oh seetroñ
lemonade
la limonade
leemo-nad
milk
le lait
leh
shandy
le panaché
pana-shay
soft drink
la boisson non alcoolisée
bwahsoñ noñ alko-leezay
with milk
au lait
oh leh

See also ACCIDENTS - CARS, BREAKDOWNS, CAR PARTS, PETROL
STATION, POLICE, ROAD SIGNS

Speed limits are 60km/h in towns, 90km/h on ordinary roads,
110 on dual carriageways and main thoroughfares, and 130
on autoroutes.

What is the speed limit on this road?
Sur cette route, la vitesse est limitée à
combien?
*soor set root la veetess eh leemee-tay a
kōñ-byāñ*

Are seat belts compulsory? Est-ce que
les ceintures de sécurité sont
obligatoires?
*es kuh lay sāñtoor duh saykoo-reetay
sōñ oblee-gatwahr*

Is there a toll on this motorway? Est-ce
que c'est une autoroute à péage?
es kuh seh oon ohtoh-root a pay-yazh

What is causing this hold-up? Quelle est
la cause de ce bouchon?
kel eh la kohz duh suh booshōñ

Is there a short-cut? Est-ce qu'il y a un
raccourci?
es keel ya ūñ rakoor-see

Where can I park? Où est-ce que je
peux me garer?
oo es kuh zhuh puh muh garay

Is there a car park nearby? Est-ce qu'il y
a un parking près d'ici?
es keel ya ūñ parking preh deesee

How long can I stay here? Je peux rester
ici combien de temps?
zhuh puh restay eesee kōñ-byāñ duh tōñ

Do I need a parking disk? Est-ce qu'il
faut un disque de stationnement?
es keel foh ūñ deesk duh sta-syon-mōñ

bend
le virage
veerazh

driving licence
le permis de
conduire
*pehrmee duh
kōñdweer*

major road
la route nationale
root na-syo-nal

minor road
la route secon-
daire
root suhgōñ-dehr

motorway
une autoroute
ohtoh-root

one-way
à sens unique
a sōñs ooneek

parking meter
le parc-mètre
park-metr

parking ticket
la contravention
kōñtra-vōñ-syōñ

sign
le panneau
panoh

traffic lights
les feux de
signalisation
*fuh duh see-
nyalee-za-syōñ*

See also DRINKS, FOOD, ORDERING, PAYING, TIPPING

Set-price menus such as *plat du jour* are often value for money.
Menus touristiques in places obviously catering for tourists
may not always be of the highest standard.

Is there a restaurant/café near here? Y a-
t-il un restaurant/café près d'ici?
ee ateel uñ resto-roñ/kafay preh deesee

A table for four please Une table pour
quatre, s'il vous plaît
oon tabl poor katr seel voo pleh

May we see the menu? Le menu, s'il
vous plaît
luh muhnoo seel voo pleh

We'll take the set menu please Nous
prendrons le menu, s'il vous plaît
noo proñdroñ luh muhnoo seel voo pleh

We'd like a drink first Nous
commencerons par un apéritif
noo komoñs-roñ par uñn apay-reeteef

Do you have a menu for children? Avez-
vous un menu pour les enfants?
avay-voo uñ muhnoo poor layz oñfoñ

Could we have some more bread/water?
Encore du pain/de l'eau, s'il vous plaît
oñkor du pañ/duh loh seel voo pleh

We'd like a dessert Nous aimerions un
dessert
nooz aym-ryoñ uñ dessehr

The bill, please L'addition, s'il vous
plaît
ladee-syoñ seel voo pleh

Is service included? Est-ce que le
service est compris?
es kuh luh sehrvees eh koñpree

cheese
le fromage
fromazh

dessert
le dessert
dessehr

lunch
le déjeuner
day-zhuh-nay

main course
le plat principal
plʌ orañsee-pal

menu
le menu
muhnoo

restaurant
le restaurant
resto-roñ

sandwich
le sandwich
soñdweech

soup
le potage
potazh

starter
un hors d'œuvre
or duhvr

terrace
la terrasse
tehras

vegetables
les légumes
laygoom

See also ACCIDENTS, BREAKDOWNS, DENTIST, DOCTOR

There's a fire! Il y a le feu!
eel ya luh fuh

Call a doctor/an ambulance! Appelez un docteur/une ambulance!
aplay uñ doktur / oon oñboo-loñs

We must get him to hospital Il faut le transporter à l'hôpital
eel foh luh troñspor-tay a lopee-tal

Fetch help quickly! Allez chercher de l'aide, vite!
alay shershay duh led veet

He can't swim Il ne sait pas nager
eel nuh seh pa na-zhay

Get the police Appelez la police
aplay la polees

Where's the nearest police station/hospital? Où est le commissariat/l'hôpital le plus proche?
oo eh luh komee-saree-a / lopee-tal luh ploo prosh

I've lost my credit card/wallet J'ai perdu ma carte de crédit/mon portefeuille
zhay pehrdoo ma kart duh kraydee / moñ port-fuhy

My child/handbag is missing Mon enfant/Mon sac a disparu
mon oñfoñ / moñ sak a deespa-roo

My passport/watch has been stolen On m'a volé mon passeport/ma montre
oñ ma volay moñ paspor / ma moñtr

I've forgotten my ticket/my key J'ai oublié mon billet/ma clé
zhay ooblee-ay moñ bee-yay / ma klay

coastguard le garde-côte
gard-koht

consulate le consulat
koñsoo-la

embassy l'ambassade
oñba-sad

fire brigade les pompiers
poñ-pyay

fire! au feu!
oh fuh

help! au secours!
oh suhkoor

lost property office le bureau des objets trouvés
booroh dayz ob-zhay troovay

police station le commissariat (de police)
komee-saroc a (duh polees)

police! police!
polees

stop thief! au voleur!
oh volur

See also NIGHTLIFE, SIGHTSEEING

Are there any local festivals? Est-ce qu'il y a des festivités locales?
es keel ya day festee-veetay lo-kal

Can you recommend something for the children? Pouvez-vous recommander quelque chose pour les enfants?
poovay-voo ruhko-mōñday kelkuh shohz poor layz ōñfōñ

What is there to do in the evenings? Qu'est-ce qu'il y a à faire le soir?
kes keel ya a fehr luh swahr

Where is there a cinema/theatre? Où est-ce qu'il y a un cinéma/théâtre?
oo es keel ya ūñ seenay-ma / tayatr

Where can we go to a concert? Où est-ce qu'on peut assister à un concert?
oo es kōñ puh asees-tay a ūñ kōñsehr

Can you book the tickets for us? Pouvez-vous nous réserver les billets?
poovay-voo noo rayzehr-vay lay bee-yay

Are there any night clubs? Y a-t-il des boîtes de nuit?
ee ateel day bwaht duh nwee

Is there a swimming pool? Est-ce qu'il y a une piscine?
es keel ya oon peeseen

Can we go fishing/riding? Est-ce qu'on peut pêcher/faire du cheval?
es kōñ puh payshay / fehr doo shuhval

Where can we play tennis/golf? Où est-ce qu'on peut faire du tennis/golf?
oo es kōñ puh fehr doo tenees / golf

Can we hire the equipment? Est-ce qu'on peut louer le matériel?
es kōñ puh loo-ay luh matay-ryel

admission charge	l'entrée *ōñtray*
bar	le bar *bar*
booking office	le bureau de location *booroh duh loka-syōñ*
club	le club *club*
disco	la discothèque *deesko-tek*
fun fair	la fête foraine *fet fo-ren*
jazz	le jazz *jaz*
orchestra	un orchestre *orkestr*
play	la pièce *pyess*
show	le spectacle *spektakl*
ticket	le billet *bee-yay*

What time is the next sailing? La prochaine traversée est à quelle heure? *la proshen travehr-say eh a kel ur*

A return ticket for one car, two adults and two children Un aller-retour pour une voiture, 2 adultes et 2 enfants *ũnn alay-ruhtoor poor oon vwatoor duhz adoolt ay duhz õnfõn*

How long does the crossing take? La traversée dure combien de temps? *la travehr-say door kõn-byãn duh tõn*

Are there any cabins/reclining seats? Est-ce qu'il y a des cabines/sièges inclinables? *es keel ya day kabeen / syezh ãnklee-nabl*

Is there a TV lounge/a bar? Est-ce qu'il y a une salle de télé/un bar? *es keel ya oon sal duh taylay / ũn bar*

Where are the toilets? Où sont les toilettes? *oo sõn lay twalet*

Where is the duty-free shop? Où est la boutique hors-taxe? *oo eh la booteek or-taks*

Can we go out on deck? Est-ce qu'on peut sortir sur le pont? *es kõn puh sorteer soor luh põn*

What is the sea like today? La mer est comment, aujourd'hui? *la mehr eh komõn oh-zhoordwee*

captain le capitaine *kapee-ten*

crew l'équipage *aykee-pazh*

hovercraft un aéroglisseur *a-ehro-gleesur*

life jacket le gilet de sauvetage *zheeleh duh sohvtazh*

lifeboat le canot de sauvetage *kanoh duh sohvtazh*

purser le commissaire du bord *komee-sehr doo bor*

rough agité *a-zheetay*

ship le bateau *batoh*

smooth calme *kalm*

the Channel la Manche *la mõnsh*

beef	**kidneys**	**pork**
le bœuf	les rognons	le porc
buhf	*ro-nyon*	*por*
bread	**kilo**	**pound**
le pain	le kilo	la livre
pan	*keeloh*	*leevr*
butter	**lamb**	**rice**
le beurre	l'agneau	le riz
buhr	*a-nyoh*	*ree*
cheese	**litre**	**salt**
le fromage	le litre	le sel
fromazh	*leetr*	*sel*
chicken	**liver**	**soup**
le poulet	le foie	le potage
pooleh	*fwah*	*potazh*
coffee	**margarine**	**steak**
le café	la margarine	le bifteck
kafay	*marga-reen*	*beeftek*
cream	**milk**	**sugar**
la crème	le lait	le sucre
krem	*leh*	*sookr*
eggs	**mince**	**tea**
les œufs	le bifteck haché	le thé
uh	*beeftek ashay*	*tay*
fish	**mustard**	**tin**
le poisson	la moutarde	la boîte
pwahson	*mootard*	*bwaht*
flour	**oil**	**veal**
la farine	l'huile	le veau
fareen	*weel*	*voh*
ham	**pasta**	**vinegar**
le jambon	les pâtes	le vinaigre
zhonbon	*paht*	*veenaygr*
jam	**pepper**	**yoghurt**
la confiture	le poivre	le yaourt
konfee-toor	*pwahvr*	*ya-oort*

apples
les pommes
pom

asparagus
les asperges
asperzh

aubergine
une aubergine
ohbehr-zheen

avocado
un avocat
avo-ka

bananas
les bananes
banan

beetroot
la betterave
betrav

carrots
les carottes
karot

cauliflower
le chou-fleur
shoo-flur

celery
le céleri
sayluh-ree

cherries
les cerises
suhreez

courgettes
les courgettes
koor-zhet

cucumber
le concombre
kōnkōnbr

french beans
les haricots verts
aree-koh vehr

garlic
l'ail
eye

grapefruit
le pamplemousse
pōnpluh-moos

grapes
les raisins
rezān

leeks
les poireaux
pwahroh

lemon
le citron
seetrōn

lettuce
la laitue
laytoo

melon
le melon
muhlōn

mushrooms
les champignons
shōnpee-nyōn

olives
les olives
oleev

onions
les oignons
o-nyōn

oranges
les oranges
orōnzh

peaches
les pêches
pesh

pears
les poires
pwahr

peas
les petits pois
puhtee pwah

pepper
le poivron
pwahvrōn

pineapple
un ananas
ana-na

plums
les prunes
proon

potatoes
les pommes de
terre
pom duh tehr

radishes
les radis
radee

raspberries
les framboises
frōnbwahz

spinach
les épinards
aypee-nar

strawberries
les fraises
frez

tomatoes
les tomates
tomat

Where can we buy souvenirs of the cathedral? Où est-ce qu'on peut acheter des souvenirs de la cathédrale?
oo es kōn puh ashtay day soov-neer duh la katay-dral

Where is the nearest gift shop? Où est la boutique de souvenirs la plus proche?
oo eh la booteek duh soov-neer la ploo prosh

I want to buy a present for my husband/wife Je voudrais acheter un cadeau pour mon mari/ma femme
zhuh voodray ashtay ūn kadoh poor mōn maree/ma fam

What is the local speciality? Quelle est la spécialité locale?
kel eh la spay-sya-leetay lo-kal

Is this hand-made? C'est fait à la main?
seh feh a la mān

I want something cheaper/more expensive Je voudrais quelque chose de moins cher/de plus cher
zhuh voodray kelkuh shohz duh mwān shehr/duh ploo shehr

Will this cheese/wine travel well? Est-ce que ce fromage/vin supporte bien le voyage?
es kuh suh fromazh/vān sooport byān luh vwah-yazh

Do you have any postcards/a guide book? Avez-vous des cartes postales/un guide?
avay-voo day kart pos-tal/ūn geed

Please wrap it up for me Enveloppez-le-moi, s'il vous plaît
ōn-vlopay-luh-mwah seel voo pleh

bracelet
le bracelet
braslay

brooch
la broche
brosh

chocolates
les chocolats
shoko-la

earrings
les boucles d'oreille
bookl doray

flowers
les fleurs
flur

necklace
le collier
ko-lyay

ornament
le bibelot
beebloh

perfume
le parfum
parfūn

pottery
la poterie
potree

ring
la bague
bag

table linen
le linge de table
lānzh duh tabl

watch
la montre
mōntr

Nouns

In French, all nouns are either **masculine** or **feminine**. Where in English we say 'the apple' and 'the book', in French it is *la pomme* and *le livre* because *pomme* is feminine and *livre* is masculine.

The gender of nouns is shown in the 'article' (=words for 'the' and 'a') used before them:

	WORDS FOR 'THE'	WORDS FOR 'A'
masculine	le, l' (*before a vowel:* l'avion)	un
feminine	la, l' (*before a vowel:* l'eau)	une

To form the **plural** of most nouns in French, an **-s** is added to the singular, as in English. But unlike English, the **-s** is not pronounced. The form 'the' for plural nouns in French, regardless of gender, is **les**, hence:

    les livres (*the books*)   **les** pommes (*the apples*)
    lay leevr   *lay pom*

NOTE: When used after the words à (*to, at*) and de (*of, from*), the words **le** and **les** contract as follows:

    à+le → **au** *oh*   de+le → **du** *doo*
    à+les → **aux** *oh*   de+les → **des** *day*

    e.g. **au** cinéma (*to the cinema*)
    le prix **du** billet (*the price of the ticket*)

'This', 'That', 'These', 'Those'

Again these depend on the gender and number of the noun they precede:

    ce livre (*this* or *that book*)
    cette pomme (*this* or *that apple*)
    ces livres/pommes (*these* or *those books/apples*)

The distinction between *this/these* and *that/those* can be made by adding **-ci** or **-là** to the noun:

    ce livre-**ci** (*this book*)   ce livre-**là** (*that book*).

Adjectives

Adjectives normally *follow* the noun they describe in French, e.g. la pomme verte (*the green apple*). Some common exceptions which *precede* the noun are:

beau *beautiful*, **bon** *good*, **grand** *big*, **gros** *big*, **haut** *high*, **jeune** *young*, **long** *long*, **joli** *pretty*, **mauvais** *bad*, **nouveau** *new*, **petit** *small*, **vieux** *old*.

French adjectives have to reflect the gender of the noun they describe. To make an adjective **feminine,** an **-e** is added to the masculine form (where this does not already end in **-e**). The masculine form is the form found in the dictionary. A final consonant usually silent in the masculine form is pronounced in the feminine, thus:

masc. le livre **vert**
luh leevr vehr
(the green book)

fem. la pomme **verte**
la pom vehrt
(the green apple)

To make an adjective **plural** an **-s** is added to the singular form, but not sounded:

masc. les livres **verts**
lay leevr vehr
(the green books)

fem. les pommes **vertes**
lay pom vehrt
(the green apples)

'My', 'Your', 'His', 'Her'

These words also depend on the gender and number of the following noun and *not* on the sex of the 'owner':

	with masc. noun	with fem. noun	with plural nouns
my	**mon** (*mōn*)	**ma** (*ma*)	**mes** (*may*)
your	**votre** (*votr*)	**votre** (*votr*)	**vos** (*voh*)
his/her*	**son** (*sōn*)	**sa** (*sa*)	**ses** (*say*)

*NOTE: There is no distinction between 'his' and 'her':
    le billet → son billet (whether the owner is 'he' or 'she').

Pronouns

SUBJECT		OBJECT	
I	**je, j'** *(before vowel) zhuh*	me	**me, m'** *muh*
you	**vous** *voo*	you	**vous** *voo*
he/it	**il** *eel*	him/it	**le, l'** *luh*
she/it	**elle** *el*	her/it	**la, l'** *la*
we	**nous** *noo*	us	**nous** *noo*
they *(masc)*	**ils** *eel*	them	**les** *lay*
(fem)	**elles** *el*		

NOTES: 1. Object pronouns are placed *before* the verb:

il (he) **vous** (you) **aime**
he loves you
nous (we) **la** (her) **connaissons**
we know her

However, in commands or requests, the pronouns *follow* the verb, as in English:
écoutez-**le**
listen to him
aidez-**moi***
help me

(But in commands expressed in the *negative*, e.g. *don't do it*, the pronouns precede the verb: ne **le** faites pas *don't do it*)

2. The object pronouns shown above are used to mean *to me, to us* etc., except:
le and **la** become **lui** *(lwee)*
les becomes **leur** *(lur)*:
e.g. **il** (he) **le** (it) **lui** (to him) **donne**
    he gives it to him

*This stressed form of **me** is used after the verb.

Verbs

There are three main patterns of endings for verbs in French - those ending -er, -ir and -re in the dictionary:

donner to give	**finir** to finish	**répondre** to reply
je donne I give	**je finis** I finish	**je réponds** I reply
zhuh don	*zhuh feenee*	*zhuh raypōn*
vous donnez you give	**vous finissez** you finish	**vous répondez** you reply
voo donay	*voo feenee-say*	*voo raypōn-day*
il/elle donne he/she gives	**il/elle finit** he/she finishes	**il/elle répond** he/she replies
eel/el don	*eel/el feenee*	*eel/el raypōn*
nous donnons we give	**nous finissons** we finish	**nous répondons** we reply
noo donōn	*noo feenee-sōn*	*noo raypōn-dōn*
ils/elles donnent they give	**ils/elles finissent** they finish	**ils/elles répondent** they reply
eel/el don	*eel/el feenees*	*eel/el raypōnd*

And in the past:

j'ai donné I gave	**j'ai fini** I finished	**j'ai répondu** I replied
zhay donay	*zhay feenee*	*zhay raypōn-doo*

For the rest of this tense, see **avoir** below

Three of the most common verbs are irregular:

être to be	**avoir** to have	**aller** to go
je suis I am	**j'ai** I have	**je vais** I go
zhuh swee	*zhay*	*zhuh vay*
vous êtes you are	**vous avez** you have	**vous allez** you go
vooz et	*vooz avay*	*vooz alay*
il/elle est he/she is	**il/elle a** he/she has	**il/elle va** he/she goes
eel/el eh	*eel/el a*	*eel/el va*
nous sommes we are	**nous avons** we have	**nous allons** we go
noo som	*nooz avōn*	*nooz alōn*
ils/elles sont they are	**ils/elles ont** they have	**ils/elles vont** they go
eel/el sōn	*eelz/elz ōn*	*eel/el vōn*

You should bear in mind that the French are rather formal when addressing each other. The familiar *tu* (you) form is used sparingly, i.e. only when you are speaking to someone you know really well. The normal form of 'you' is *vous*. Also widely used are *Monsieur, Madame* and *Mademoiselle*. To greet, for instance, a Madame Courtin whom you do not know, or whom you have met only a few times before, you should say 'Bonjour, Madame', not just 'Bonjour' or 'Bonjour, Madame Courtin'. Remember too that shaking hands is normal when greeting and taking leave, and is not restricted to the first meeting.

Hello Bonjour
boñ-zhoor

Good morning/Good afternoon Bonjour
boñ-zhoor

Good evening Bonsoir
boñswahr

Goodbye Au revoir
oh ruhvwahr

Good night Bonsoir
boñswahr

How do you do? Enchanté (de faire votre connaissance)
oñshoñ-tay (duh fehr votr koneh-soñs)

Pleased to meet you Enchanté
oñshoñ-tay

How nice to see you Je suis ravi de vous voir
zhuh swee ravee duh voo vwahr

How are you? Comment ça va?
komoñ sa va

Fine thank you Très bien, merci
treh byañ mehrsee

See you soon A bientôt
a byañtoh

See you later (*in the day*) A tout à l'heure
a toot a lur

I'd like to make an appointment Je voudrais prendre rendez-vous
zhuh voodray prōndr rōnday-voo

A cut and blow-dry please Coupe et brushing, s'il vous plaît
koop ay bruhshing seel voo pleh

A shampoo and set Shampooing et mise en plis
shōnpwan ay meez ōn plee

Not too short Pas trop court
pa troh koor

I'd like it layered Je voudrais une coupe en dégradé
zhuh voodray oon koop ōn daygra-day

Not too much off the back/the fringe Ne coupez pas trop derrière/la frange
nuh koopay pa troh deh-ryehr/la frōnzh

Take more off the top/the sides Un peu plus court sur le dessus/les côtés
ūn puh ploo koor soor luh duhsoo/lay kohtay

My hair is permed/tinted J'ai une permanente/une coloration
zhay oon pehrma-nōnt/oon kolo-ra-syōn

My hair is naturally curly/straight Mes cheveux frisent/sont raides naturellement
may shuhvuh freez/sōn red natoo-relmōn

It's too hot C'est trop chaud
seh troh shoh

I'd like a conditioner please Un après-shampooing, s'il vous plaît
ūnn apreh-shōnpwan seel voo pleh

gown
le peignoir
peny-wahr

hair cut
la coupe
koop

hair spray
la laque
lak

long
long
lōn

parting
la raie
ray

perm
une permanente
pehrma-nōnt

shampoo
le shampooing
shōnpwan

short
court
koor

streaks
les mèches
mesh

styling mousse
le fixateur
feeksa-tur

towel
la serviette
sehr-vyet

trim, to
rafraîchir
rafreh-sheer

See also ACCOMMODATION, ROOM SERVICE, PAYING

I reserved a room in the name of ... J'ai
réservé une chambre au nom de ...
zhay rayzehr-vay oon shoñbr oh noñ duh

**I confirmed my booking by phone/by
letter** J'ai confirmé ma réservation par
téléphone/lettre
*zhay koñfeer-may ma rayzehr-va-syoñ
par taylay-fon/letr*

Could you have my luggage taken up?
Vous pouvez faire monter mes
bagages?
voo poovay fehr moñtay may bagazh

What time is breakfast/dinner? Le petit
déjeuner/Le dîner est à quelle heure?
*luh puhtee day-zhuh-nay/luh deenay eh
a kel ur*

**Can we have a packed lunch for our
picnic?** Est-ce que nous pouvons avoir
un panier-repas pour notre pique-
nique?
*es kuh noo poovoñ avwahr uñ pa-nyay-
ruhpa poor notr peek-neek*

Please call me at seven thirty Réveillez-
moi à 7.30, s'il vous plaît
*rayvay-yay-mwah a set ur troñt seel voo
pleh*

My key, please Ma clé, s'il vous plaît
ma klay seel voo pleh

I want to stay an extra night Je voudrais
rester une nuit supplémentaire
*zhuh voodray restay oon nwee sooplay-
moñtehr*

**I shall be leaving at 8 o'clock tomorrow
morning** Je partirai demain matin à 8
heures
zhuh partee-ray duhmañ matañ a weet ur

bar	le bar
	bar
desk	la réception
	raysep-syoñ
lift	un ascenseur
	asoñ-sur
lounge	le salon
	saloñ
manager	le directeur
	deerek-tur
porter	le porteur
	portur
reservation	la réservation
	rayzehr-va-syoñ
restaurant	le restaurant
	resto-roñ
room service	le service des chambres
	sehrvees day shoñbr
stay	le séjour
	say-zhoor
TV lounge	la salle de télévision
	sal duh taylay-vee-zyoñ

Where do I check in my luggage? Où est-ce qu'on enregistre les bagages? *oo es kôn ônruh-zheestr lay bagazh*

Where is the luggage from the London flight/train? Où sont les bagages du vol/train en provenance de Londres? *oo sôn lay bagazh doo vol/trân ôn provnôns duh lôndr*

Our luggage has not arrived Nos bagages ne sont pas arrivés *noh bagazh nuh sôn pa aree-vay*

My suitcase was damaged in transit Ma valise a été endommagée pendant le voyage *ma valeez a aytay ôndo-ma-zhay pôndôn luh vwah-yazh*

Where is the left luggage office? Où est la consigne? *oo eh la kônsee-nyuh*

Are there any luggage trolleys? Est-ce qu'il y a des chariots pour les bagages? *es keel ya day sha-ryoh poor lay bagazh*

My case is very heavy Ma valise est très lourde *ma valeez eh treh loord*

Can you help me with my bags please? Est-ce que vous pouvez m'aider à porter mes bagages? *es kuh voo poovay meday a portay may bagazh*

Please take my bags to a taxi Est-ce que vous pouvez porter mes bagages jusqu'à un taxi? *es kuh voo poovay portay may bagazh zhooska ûn taxi*

I sent my luggage on in advance J'ai envoyé mes bagages à l'avance *zhay ônvwah-yay may bagazh a lavôns*

baggage reclaim la réception des bagages *raysep-syôn day bagazh*

excess luggage l'excédent de bagages *eksay-dôn duh bagazh*

flight bag le sac avion *sak a-vyôn*

hand luggage les bagages à main *bagazh a mân*

locker le casier à consigne automatique *ka-zyay a kônsee-nyuh ohtoh-mateek*

luggage allowance le poids maximum autorisé *pwah maksee-mom oto-reezay*

luggage rack le porte-bagages *port-bagazh*

porter le porteur *portur*

trunk la malle *mal*

See also DIRECTIONS

Where can I buy a local map? Où est-ce que je peux acheter une carte de la région?
oo es kuh zhuh puh ashtay oon kart duh la ray-zhyoñ

Have you got a town plan? Est-ce que vous avez un plan de la ville?
es kuh vooz avay uñ ploñ duh la veel

I want a street map of the city Je voudrais un plan de la ville
zhuh voodray uñ ploñ duh la veel

I need a road map of ... J'ai besoin d'une carte routière de ...
zhay buhzwañ doon kart roo-tyehr duh ...

Can I get a map at the tourist office? Est-ce que je peux obtenir un plan au syndicat d'initiative?
es kuh zhuh puh optuh-neer uñ ploñ oh sañdee-ka deenee-sya-teev

Can you show me on the map? Est-ce que vous pouvez me montrer sur la carte?
es kuh voo poovay muh moñtray soor la kart

Do you have a guide book in English? Est-ce que vous avez un guide touristique en anglais?
es kuh vooz avay uñ geed toorees-teek oñn oñgleh

Do you have a guide book to the cathedral? Est-ce que vous avez un guide sur la cathédrale?
es kuh vooz avay uñ geed soor la katay-dral

I need an English-French dictionary J'ai besoin d'un dictionnaire anglais-français
zhay buhzwañ duñ deek-syo-nehr oñgleh-froñseh

Do you have an English phrase book? Est-ce que vous avez un manuel de conversation anglaise?
es kuh vooz avay uñ manwel duh koñvehr-sa-syoñ oñglez

See also BUYING, CONVERSION CHARTS, NUMBERS, PAYING

a pint of ...
un demi-litre de ...
ūn duhmee leetr duh

a litre of ...
un litre de ...
ūn leetr duh

a kilo of ...
un kilo de ...
ūn keeloh duh

a pound of ...
une livre de ...
oon leevr duh

100 grammes of ...
cent grammes de ...
sōn gram duh

half a kilo of ...
une livre de ...
oon leevr duh

a half-bottle of ...
une demi-bouteille de ...
oon duhmee-bootay duh

a slice of ...
une tranche de ...
oon trōnsh duh

a portion of ...
une portion de ...
oon por-syōn duh

a dozen ...
une douzaine de ...
oon doozen duh

150 francs worth of ...
pour 150 francs de ...
poor sōn-sānkōnt frōn duh

a third
un tiers
ūn tyehr

two thirds
deux tiers
duh tyehr

a quarter
un quart
ūn kar

three quarters
trois quarts
trwah kar

ten per cent
dix pour cent
dee poor sōn

more
plus
ploos

less
moins
mwān

enough
assez
assay

double
le double
luh doobluh

twice
deux fois
duh fwah

three times
trois fois
trwah fwah

See also EATING OUT, FOOD, WINES AND SPIRITS, WINE LIST

Starters - Entrées, hors d'œuvres

Artichauts à la vinaigrette artichokes with vinaigrette
Asperges à l'huile asparagus with vinaigrette
Assiette anglaise assorted cold meats
Champignons à la grecque mushrooms in oil, wine and herbs
Crevettes grises au beurre potted shrimps
Crudités selection of salads and raw vegetables
Cuisses de grenouille frogs' legs
Escargots snails
Foie gras (d'oie) (goose) liver pâté
Fonds d'artichauts artichoke hearts
Huîtres oysters
Jambon de Bayonne raw cured ham (from the Basque
Country)
Jambon de Parme Parma ham
Œuf mayonnaise egg mayonnaise
Pointes d'asperges asparagus tips
Saumon fumé (d'Ecosse) (Scotch) smoked salmon
Terrine maison pâté maison

Soups - Potages

Bouillabaisse soup/stew made with fish and shellfish, a
speciality of Marseilles
Consommé de poulet chicken consommé, clear chicken soup
Crème de tomates cream of tomato soup
Potage à l'oseille sorrel soup
Potage Saint-Germain split-pea soup served with croutons
Soupe à l'oignon onion soup served with croutons
Velouté de poireaux et pommes de terre (cream of) leek and
potato soup

Fish and seafood - Poissons et fruits de mer

Anguille eel
Brochet pike
Cabillaud au gratin cod, bechamel sauce and cheese topping
Coquilles Saint-Jacques scallops
Daurade à la crème sea bream in a cream sauce with mushrooms
Filet de sole meunière sole cooked in butter, served with lemon
Homard à l'armoricaine/à l'américaine lobster sautéed with shallots, tomatoes and white wine; sometimes brandy is added
Langouste crayfish
Langoustines scampi
Lotte farcie stuffed turbot
Maquereau au vin blanc mackerel in white wine
Morue salt cod
Moules marinières mussels in white wine
Raie au beurre noir skate in black butter
Saumon grillé grilled salmon
Thon tuna
Truite aux amandes trout cooked in butter and chopped almonds

Poultry - Volailles

Canard à l'orange roast duck stuffed with orange, served with an orange and wine sauce
Caneton rôti roast duckling
Confit d'oie goose cooked and preserved in its own fat
Coq au vin chicken cooked in red wine
Faisan pheasant
Perdreau partridge
Pintadeau guinea fowl
Poule au riz boiled chicken with rice
Poulet basquaise chicken pieces cooked with tomatoes, peppers, mushrooms, diced ham and white wine

Meat dishes - Viandes

Andouille tripe sausage
Bifteck steak
Blanquette de veau stewed veal in a white sauce
Bœuf bourguignon beef stew with red wine
Bœuf en daube beef casserole
Boudin (noir) black (blood) pudding
Carré d'agneau loin of lamb
Cassoulet bean stew with pork or mutton and sausages
Cervelles brains
Choucroute garnie sauerkraut garnished with assorted pork meats and boiled potatoes
Civet de lièvre jugged hare
Côtelettes de veau veal cutlets
Côtes de porc pork chops
Entrecôte grillée grilled rib steak
Epaule d'agneau shoulder of lamb
Escalope panée veal escalope in breadcrumbs
Faux-filet sirloin
Gigot d'agneau leg of lamb
Hachis parmentier French version of shepherd's pie
Lapin chasseur rabbit cooked in white wine and herbs
Paupiettes de veau veal olives
Pot au feu boiled beef and vegetables
Râble de lièvre roast saddle of hare
Ragoût de mouton mutton stew
Ris de veau sweetbreads
Rognons sautés au madère sautéed kidneys in madeira sauce
Rôti de bœuf/porc roast beef/pork
Steak au poivre pepper steak
Tournedos fillet steak
Tripes à la mode de Caen tripe with vegetables, herbs, cider and calvados

Salads and vegetable dishes - Salades et légumes

Aubergines farcies stuffed aubergines
Carottes râpées grated carrot in vinaigrette
Carottes Vichy carrots cooked in sugar and butter
Céleri rémoulade shredded celery roots in mayonnaise and mustard
Champignons en salade sliced raw mushrooms in vinaigrette
Piperade cooked tomatoes and pimentos in an omelette mixture
Pommes à l'anglaise boiled potatoes
Pommes dauphine potato croquettes
Pommes frites chips/French fries
Salade de pommes de terre cold boiled potatoes in vinaigrette
Salade (verte) green salad with vinaigrette
Salade niçoise mixed salad with French beans, tomatoes, peppers, potatoes, olives, anchovies

Cheese board - Le plateau de fromages, Les fromages

The cheese course normally comes straight after the main dish in France.

Bleu de Bresse mild blue-veined cheese with a soft texture
Brie soft and creamy, one of the best-known French cheeses
Camembert probably the best-known cheese of all. Soft and well-flavoured, it is pungent when fully ripened
Cantal semi-hard, fairly strong flavoured cheese
Chèvre goat's milk cheese; there are many varieties
Comté a hard cheese from Jura, with a tangy taste
Coulommiers similar to Brie, soft and creamy
Emmenthal from Switzerland, similar to Gruyère
Gruyère hard Swiss cheese with a delicate flavour
Petit Suisse small pots of rich, creamy-soft cheese
Pont-l'évêque softish, mature, square-shaped cheese
Roquefort blue-veined cheese made from ewe's milk
Saint Paulin large round cheese made from rich cow's milk
Tomme aux raisins semi-soft cheese covered with grape pips

Desserts and cakes - Desserts et gâteaux

Baba au rhum rum baba
Beignets de pommes apple fritters
Chou à la crème cream puff
Clafoutis pastry or batter pudding filled with black cherries
Coupe de fruits fruit salad
Crème caramel caramel custard
Crème renversée caramelized custard
Crêpe pancake
Dacquoise meringue dessert with fruit and cream
Eclair eclair
Flan egg custard
Glace à la vanille/au chocolat vanilla/chocolate ice cream
Mille-feuilles vanilla slice
Mousse au chocolat chocolate mousse
Profiteroles small cream puffs
Salade de fruits fruit salad
Savarin rum-soaked cake
Tarte aux mirabelles/aux raisins plum/grape open tart
Tarte tatin upside-down apple tart
Vacherin meringue or almond base with ice-cream and Chantilly
Yaourt yoghurt

Snacks

Chips crisps
Crêpe pancake
Croque-Monsieur toasted ham and cheese sandwich
Frites chips
Gauffre waffle
Marrons grillés roasted chestnuts
Sandwich au jambon ham sandwich (in French bread)
Saucisses sausages

Understanding the menu

à l'ail with garlic
à la crème with cream
à la vanille vanilla(-flavoured)
au café/chocolat coffee/chocolate(-flavoured)
au four oven-baked
aux fraises/framboises with strawberries/raspberries
au gratin with a cheese topping
au vin (rouge) in (red) wine
au vin blanc in white wine
en gelée in aspic
farci stuffed
frit fried
garni with vegetables or rice accompaniment
grillé grilled
pané in breadcrumbs
provençale cooked in olive oil with herbs, tomatoes and olives
vinaigrette French dressing, vinaigrette; served in vinaigrette

Types of bread and buns

baguette long thin loaf
brioche sweet roll
croissant yeast-risen pastry
pain standard large loaf
pain au chocolat chocolate-filled bun
pain d'épices spicy cake (similar to gingerbread)

I haven't enough money Je n'ai pas assez d'argent
zhuh nay pa assay dar-zhōn

Have you any change? Est-ce que vous avez de la monnaie?
es kuh vooz avay duh la monay

Can you change a 50 franc note? Est-ce que vous avez la monnaie de 50 francs?
es kuh vooz avay la monay duh sāṅkōnt frōn

I'd like to change these traveller's cheques Je voudrais changer ces travellers
zhuh voodray shōn-zhay say travuh-lurz

I want to change some francs into pounds Je voudrais changer des francs en livres
zhuh voodray shōn-zhay day frōn ōn leevr

What is the rate for sterling/dollars? Combien vaut la livre/le dollar?
kōn-byān voh la leevr / luh dollar

Can I get a cash advance with my credit card? Est-ce que je peux obtenir de l'argent liquide avec ma carte de crédit?
es kuh zhuh puh optuh-neer duh lar-zhōn leekeed avek ma kart duh kraydee

I should like to transfer some money from my bank in ... Je voudrais transférer de l'argent de ma banque à...
zhuh voodray trōnsfay-ray duh lar-zhōn duh ma bōnk a ...

How much? Combien?
kōn-byān

account
le compte
kōnt
bank
la banque
bōnk
bureau de change
le bureau de change
booroh duh shōnzh
cash
l'argent liquide
ar-zhōn leekeed
cheque book
le carnet de chèques
karneh duh shek
currency
les devises étrangères
duhveez aytrōn-zhehr
exchange rate
le taux de change
toh duh shōnzh
notes
les billets (de banque)
bee-yay (duh bōnk)
post office
le bureau de poste
booroh duh post
purse
le porte-monnaie
port-monay
wallet
le portefeuille
port-fuhy

See also EATING OUT, ENTERTAINMENT

What is there to do in the evenings? Qu'est-ce qu'on peut faire le soir?
kes koñ puh fehr luh swahr

Where can we go to dance/to see a cabaret? Où est-ce qu'on peut aller danser/voir un spectacle de cabaret?
oo es koñ puh alay doñsay/vwahr uñ spekta-kluh duh kaba-reh

Are there any good night clubs/discos? Est-ce qu'il y a de bonnes boîtes de nuit/de bonnes discos?
es keel ya duh bon bwaht duh nwee/duh bon deeskoh

How do we get to the casino? Pour aller au casino, s'il vous plaît?
poor alay oh kazee-noh seel voo pleh

Do we need to be members? Est-ce qu'il faut être membre?
es keel foh etr moñbr

How much does it cost to get in? L'entrée coûte combien?
loñtray koot koñ-byañ

We'd like to reserve two seats for tonight Nous désirons réserver 2 places pour ce soir
noo dayzee-roñ rayzehr-vay duh plas poor suh swahr

Is there a bar/a restaurant? Est-ce qu'il y a un bar/un restaurant?
es keel ya uñ bar/uñ resto-roñ

What time does the show/concert begin? Le spectacle/concert commence à quelle heure?
luh spekta-kluh/koñsehr komoñs a kel ur

How long does the performance last? Le spectacle dure combien de temps?
luh spekta-kluh door koñ-byañ duh toñ

Which film is on at the cinema? Quel film passe au cinéma?
kel feelm pas oh seenay-ma

Can we get there by bus/taxi? Est-ce qu'on peut y aller en bus/taxi?
es koñ puh ee alay oñ boos/taxi

Accès aux quais
To the trains

A louer
For hire, To rent

Appuyez
Push

Arrêt
Stop

Ascenseur
Lift

A vendre
For sale

Baignade interdite
No bathing

Billets
Tickets

Caisse
Cash desk

Casse-croûte(s)
Snacks

Chambres
Rooms to let

Chaud
Hot

Complet
No vacancies

Composter votre billet
Punch your ticket here

Consigne
Left luggage

Dames
Ladies

Défense de fumer
No smoking

Défense de marcher sur les pelouses
Do not walk on the grass

Dégustation de vins
Wine tasting

Douche
Shower

Eau potable
Drinking water

En panne
Out of order

Entrée
Entrance

Fermé
Closed

Froid
Cold

Fumeurs
Smokers, Smoking

Gendarmerie
Police station

Hommes
Men

Libre
Free, Vacant

Libre-service
Self-service

Messieurs
Gentlemen, Men

Non-fumeurs
Non-smokers, No smoking

Occupé
Engaged

Ouvert
Open

Poussez
Push

Pressing
Dry cleaning

Prière de ...
Please...

Privé
Private

Renseignements
Information, Enquiries

Rez-de-chaussée
Ground floor

Soldes
Sale

Sonnez
Ring

Sortie
Exit

Sortie de secours
Emergency exit

Sous-sol
Basement

Syndicat d'initiative
Tourist Information Office

Teinturerie
Dry Cleaner's

Tirez
Pull

See also MEASUREMENTS AND QUANTITIES

0	zéro *zayroh*	13	treize *trez*	50	cinquante *sānkōnt*
1	un *ūn*	14	quatorze *katorz*	60	soixante *swasōnt*
2	deux *duh*	15	quinze *kānz*	70	soixante-dix *swasōnt-dees*
3	trois *trwah*	16	seize *sez*	80	quatre-vingts *katr-vān*
4	quatre *katr*	17	dix-sept *dee-set*	90	quatre-vingt-dix *katr-vān-dees*
5	cinq *sānk*	18	dix-huit *deez-weet*	100	cent *sōn*
6	six *sees*	19	dix-neuf *deez-nuhf*	110	cent dix *sōn dees*
7	sept *set*	20	vingt *vān*	200	deux cents *duh sōn*
8	huit *weet*	21	vingt et un *vānt ay ūn*	300	trois cents *trwah sōn*
9	neuf *nuhf*	22	vingt-deux *vān-duh*	1,000	mille *meel*
10	dix *dees*	23	vingt-trois *vān-trwah*	2,000	deux mille *duh meel*
11	onze *ōnz*	30	trente *trōnt*	1,000,000	un million *ūn mee-lyōn*
12	douze *dooz*	40	quarante *karōnt*		

1st	premier, première *pruh-myay, pruh-myehr*	6th	sixième *see-zyem*
2nd	deuxième *duh-zyem*	7th	septième *seh-tyem*
3rd	troisième *trwah-zyem*	8th	huitième *wee-tyem*
4th	quatrième *katree-yem*	9th	neuvième *nuh-vyem*
5th	cinquième *sān-kyem*	10th	dixième *dee-zyem*

See also COMPLAINTS, EATING OUT, MENUS, PAYING, WINES AND SPIRITS

Do you have a set menu? Est-ce que vous avez un menu à prix fixe?
es kuh vooz avay uñ muhnoo a pree feeks

We will have the menu at 45 francs Le menu à 45 francs
luh muhnoo a karoñt-sañk froñ

May we see the wine list, please? La carte des vins, s'il vous plaît
la kart day vañ seel voo pleh

What do you recommend? Qu'est-ce que vous nous conseillez?
kes kuh voo noo koñsay-yay

Is there a local speciality? Est-ce qu'il y a une spécialité régionale?
es keel ya oon spay-sya-leetay ray-zhonal

How is this dish served? Ce plat est servi comment?
suh pla eh sehrvee komoñ

How do I eat this? Comment ça se mange?
komoñ sa suh moñzh

What is in this dish? Ce plat est préparé avec quoi?
suh pla eh praypa-ray avek kwah

Are the vegetables included? Est-ce que les légumes sont compris?
es kuh lay laygoom soñ koñpree

Rare/Medium rare/Well done Saignant/Pas trop cuit/Bien cuit
say-nyoñ/pa troh kwee/byañ kwee

We'd like a dessert/some coffee, please Les desserts/Du café, s'il vous plaît
lay dessehr/doo kafay seel voo pleh

bill
une addition
adee-syoñ

course
le plat
pla

cover charge
le couvert
koovehr

meal
le repas
ruhpa

order
la commande
komoñd

service
le service
sehrvees

table
la table
tabl

that one
celui-là
suh-lwee-la

this one
celui-ci
suh-lwee-see

waiter
le garçon
garsoñ

waitress
la serveuse
sehrvuhz

See also BUYING, MONEY

Can I have the bill, please? L'addition,
s'il vous plaît
ladee-syõn seel voo pleh

Is service/tax included? Est-ce que le
service est compris?/Est-ce que la taxe
est comprise?
*es kuh luh sehrvees eh kõñpree/es kuh
la taks eh kõñpreez*

What does that come to? Ça fait
combien?
sa feh kõñ-byañ

Do I pay in advance? Est-ce que c'est
payable d'avance?
es kuh seh pay-yabl davõñs

Do I pay a deposit? Est-ce qu'il y a des
arrhes à verser?
es keel ya dayz ar a vehrsay

Can I pay by credit card/cheque? Est-ce
qu'il est possible de payer avec une
carte de crédit/par chèque?
*es keel eh poseebl duh pay-yay avek
oon kart duh kraydee/par shek*

Do you accept traveller's cheques? Est-
ce que vous acceptez les travellers?
es kuh vooz aksep-tay lay traveh-lurz

I don't have enough in cash Je n'ai pas
assez en liquide
zhuh nay pa assay õñ leekeed

**I think you've given me the wrong
change** Je crois que vous ne m'avez pas
rendu juste
*zhuh krwah kuh voo nuh mavay pa
rõñdoo zhoost*

I'd like a receipt, please Un reçu, s'il
vous plaît
uñ ruhsoo seel voo pleh

cash desk
la caisse
kes
cashier
le caissier (la
caissière)
*keh-syay (keh-
syehr)*
charge
le prix
pree
cheaper
moins cher
mwañ shehr
cheque card
la carte d'identité
bancaire
*kart deedõñ-teetay
bõñkehr*
discount
le rabais
rabeh
expensive
cher
shehr
payment
le paiement
paymõñ
reduction
la réduction
raydook-syõñ
signature
la signature
see-nyatoor
till
la caisse
kes

My name is ... Je m'appelle ...
zhuh mapel ...

My date of birth is 12th February 1949
Je suis né le 12 février 1949
*zhuh swee nay luh dooz fayvree-ay meel
nuf sōn karōnt-nuf*

My address is ... J'habite ...
zhabeet ...

I come from Britain/America Je suis
Britannique/Américain
zhuh swee breeta-neek / amay-reekān

I live in Manchester/Scotland J'habite à
Manchester/en Ecosse
zhabeet a manchester / ōnn aykos

My passport/driving licence number is...
Le numéro de mon passeport/permis
de conduire est ...
*luh noomay-roh duh mōn paspor /
pehrmee duh kōndweer eh ...*

I work in an office/a factory Je travaille
dans un bureau/une usine
zhuh travye dōnz ūn booroh / oon oozeen

I am a secretary/manager Je suis
secrétaire/directeur
zhuh swee suhkray-tehr / deerek-tur

I'm here on holiday/business Je suis ici
en vacances/en voyage d'affaires
*zhuh swee eesee ōn vakōns / ōn vwah-
yazh dafehr*

There are four of us altogether Nous
sommes 4
noo som katr

My daughter/son is 6 Ma fille/Mon fils a
6 ans
ma feey / mōn fees a seez ōn

blind	aveugle
	avuh-gluh
child	un enfant
	ōnfōn
deaf	sourd
	soor
disabled	handicapé
	ōndee-kapay
English	anglais
	ōngleh
husband	le mari
	maree
Irish	irlandais
	eerlōn-deh
Scottish	écossais
	ayko-seh
student	étudiant
	aytoo-dyōn
Welsh	gallois
	galwah
wife	la femme
	fam

See also CAR PARTS, DRIVING ABROAD, PAYING

20 litres of 2 star 20 litres d'ordinaire
vañ leetr dordee-nehr

100 francs (worth) of 4 star, please 100
francs de super, s'il vous plaît
soñ froñ duh soopehr seel voo pleh

Fill it up please Le plein, s'il vous plaît
luh plañ seel voo pleh

Check the oil/the water, please Vérifiez
l'huile/l'eau, s'il vous plaît
vayree-fee-ay lweel/loh seel voo pleh

Top up the windscreen washers
Remplissez les lave-glaces
roñplee-say lay lavglas

Could you clean the windscreen? Faites
le pare-brise, s'il vous plaît
fet luh parbreez seel voo pleh

Where's the air line? Où se trouve le
manomètre pour la pression des pneus?
oo suh troov luh mano-metr poor la preh-syoñ day pnuh

Can I have a can of petrol/oil? Un bidon
d'essence/d'huile, s'il vous plaît
uñ beedoñ dessoñs/dweel seel voo pleh

Is there a telephone/a lavatory? Est-ce
qu'il y a un téléphone/des toilettes?
es keel ya uñ taylay-fon/day twalet

How do I use the car wash? Comment
marche le lave-auto?
komoñ marsh luh lav-ohtoh

Can I pay by credit card? Est-ce que je
peux payer avec une carte de crédit?
*es kuh zhuh puh pay-yay avek oon kart
duh kraydee*

attendant	un employé
	oñplwah-yay
diesel	le gas-oil
	gazol
distilled water	l'eau distillée
	oh deestee-lay
garage	le garage
	garazh
hose	le tuyau
	twee-yoh
petrol pump	la pompe à
	essence
	poñp a essoñs
petrol station	la station-service
	sta-syoñ-sehrvees
tyre pressure	la pression des
	pneus
	*preh-syoñ day
	pnuh*

I need a colour/black and white film for this camera Je voudrais un film couleur/noir et blanc pour cet appareil
zhuh voodray ūn feelm koolur/nwahr ay blōn poor set apa-ray

It is for prints/slides C'est pour des photos sur papier/des diapositives
seh poor day fohtoh soor pa-pyay/day dee-apo-zeeteev

Have you got some flash cubes for this camera? Avez-vous des flashs pour cet appareil?
avay-voo day flash poor set apa-ray

There's something wrong with my cine-camera Ma caméra ne marche pas bien
ma kamay-ra nuh marsh pa byān

The film/shutter has jammed Le film/L'obturateur est bloqué
luh feelm/loptoo-ratur eh blokay

Can you develop this film? Pouvez-vous développer ce film?
poovay-voo day-vlopay suh feelm

When will the photos be ready? Les photos seront prêtes quand?
lay fohtoh suhrōn pret kōn

Can I take photos in here? Est-ce que je peux prendre des photos, ici?
es kuh zhuh puh prōndr day fohtoh eesee

Would you take a photo of us, please? Est-ce que vous pourriez prendre une photo de nous, s'il vous plaît?
es kuh voo pooree-ay prōndr oon fohtoh duh noo seel voo pleh

cartridge	
le chargeur	
shar-zhur	
cassette	
la cassette	
kasset	
exposure meter	
le posemètre	
pohzmetr	
flash	
le flash	
flash	
flash bulb	
une ampoule de flash	
ōnpool duh flash	
lens	
un objectif	
ob-zhekteef	
lens cover	
le protège-lentille	
protezh-lōnteey	
movie camera	
la caméra	
kamay-ra	
negative	
le négatif	
nayga-teef	
reel	
la bobine	
bobeen	
tripod	
le trépied	
tray-pyay	

See also ACCIDENTS, CUSTOMS AND PASSPORTS, EMERGENCIES

The police in France are vigilant and have the power to impose on-the-spot fines.

We should call the police Nous devrions appeler la police
noo duh-vryoñ aplay la polees

Where is the police station? Où est le poste de police?
oo eh luh post duh polees

Some things have been stolen from my car On a volé des choses dans ma voiture
oñ a volay day shohz doñ ma vwatoor

I've been robbed On m'a volé quelque chose
oñ ma volay kelkuh shohz

I have had an accident J'ai eu un accident
zhay oo uñn aksee-doñ

How much is the fine? L'amende est de combien?
lamoñd eh duh koñ-byañ

How do I pay it? Comment est-ce que je la paie?
komoñ es kuh zhuh la peh

I don't have my driving licence on me Je n'ai pas mon permis de conduire sur moi
zhuh nay pa moñ pehrmee duh koñdweer soor mwah

I'm very sorry, officer Je suis désolé, monsieur
zhuh swee dayzo-lay muh-syuh

I didn't know the regulations Je ne connaissais pas la réglementation
zhuh nuh koneh-seh pa la regluh-moñta-syoñ

car number le numéro de la voiture
noomay-roh duh la vwatoor

documents les papiers
pa-pyay

green card la carte verte
kart vehrt

insurance certificate la carte d'assurance (automobile)
kart dasoo-roñs (ohtoh-mobeel)

lawyer un avocat
avo-ka

police car la voiture de police
vwatoor duh polees

policeman un agent de police
a-zhoñ duh polees

traffic offence une infraction au code de la route
añfrak-syoñ oh kod duh la root

traffic warden le contractuel
koñtrak-too-el

Stamps can also be bought in *café-tabacs*, hotels and newsagents.

How much is a letter to England/America? C'est combien pour envoyer une lettre en Angleterre/Amérique?
seh koñ-byañ poor oñvwah-yay oon letr oñn oñgluh-tehr / amay-reek

Six stamps for postcards to Britain, please Six timbres pour cartes postales pour la Grande-Bretagne
see tañbr poor kart pos-tal poor la groñd-bruhta-nyuh

Twelve 3 franc stamps please Douze timbres à 3 francs, s'il vous plaît
dooz tañbr a trwah froñ seel voo pleh

I want to send a telegram to Scotland Je voudrais envoyer un télégramme en Ecosse
zhuh voodray oñvwah-yay uñ taylay-gram oñn aykos

When will it arrive? Ça arrivera quand?
sa aree-vuhra koñ

How much will it cost? Ça coûte combien?
sa koot koñ-byañ

I want to send this parcel Je voudrais envoyer ce paquet
zhuh voodray oñvwah-yay suh pakeh

I'd like to make a telephone call Je voudrais téléphoner
zhuh voodray taylay-fonay

I want to draw some money out of my Giro account Je voudrais retirer de l'argent de mon compte chèque postal britannique
zhuh voodray ruhtee-ray duh lar-zhoñ duh moñ koñt shek pos-tal breeta-neek

air mail par avion
par a-vyoñ

clerk un employé
oñplwah-yay

counter le guichet
geesheh

express exprès
ekspress

form le formulaire
formoo-lehr

international international
añtehr-na-syo-nal

money order le mandat
moñda

post office le bureau de poste
booroh duh post

postage l'affranchissement
afroñ-sheesmoñ

registered recommandé
ruhko-moñday

reply coupon le coupon-réponse
koopoñ-raypoñs

See also ACCIDENTS, COMPLAINTS, EMERGENCIES, POLICE

Can you help me, please? Est-ce que vous pouvez m'aider, s'il vous plaît?
es kuh voo poovay meday seel voo pleh

What is the matter? Qu'est-ce qu'il y a?
kes keel ya

I am in trouble J'ai un problème
zhay ūñ problem

I don't understand Je ne comprends pas
zhuh nuh kōñprōñ pa

Do you speak English? Est-ce que vous parlez anglais?
es kuh voo parlay ōñgleh

Please repeat that Répétez, s'il vous plaît
raypay-tay seel voo pleh

I have run out of money Je n'ai plus d'argent
zhuh nay ploo dar-zhōñ

My son is lost Mon fils a disparu
mōñ fees a deespa-roo

I have lost my way Je me suis perdu
zhuh muh swee pehrdoo

I have forgotten my passport J'ai oublié mon passeport
zhay ooblee-ay mōñ paspor

Please give me my passport back Mon passeport, s'il vous plaît
mōñ paspor seel voo pleh

Where is the British Consulate? Où est le consulat britannique?
oo eh luh kōñsoo-la breeta-neek

In the pronunciation system used in this book, French sounds are represented by spellings of the nearest possible sounds in English. Hence, when you read out the pronunciation, given in *italics*, sound the letters as if you were reading an English word. The following notes should help you:

REPRESENTATION	REMARKS	EXAMPLE	PRONUNCIATION
e/eh	As in *met*	**sec**	*sek*
u/uh	As in *thud*	**repas**	*ruhpa*
oh	As in *go, low*	**bateau**	*batoh*
o	As in *dot*	**colle**	*kol*
ōn	Nasalized: let air	**restaurant**	*resto-rōn*
ān	out through the	**pain**	*pān*
ūn	nose as well as the mouth	**lundi**	*lūndee*
zh	As in *measure*	**rouge**	*roozh*
y	As in *yet*	**pied**	*pyay*
ye	As in *fry*	**travail**	*tra-vye*
ny	As in *companion*	**signal**	*see-nyal*
s	As in *sit*	**police**	*polees*

Pronouncing French words from their spelling can be made easier by following some fairly precise 'rules'. Final consonants are often silent.

SPELLING	REPRESENTATION	SPELLING	REPRESENTATION
à, â	*a/ah*	ou, oû, u	*oo*
e	*e/eh* (see above)	ui, uî	*wee*
	uh (see above)	y	*ee*
é	*ay*	g (+e/i), j	*zh* (see above)
è, ê	*e/eh* (see above)	gn	*ny* (see above)
i, î	*ee*	ch	*sh*
ô	*o* (see above)	th	*t*
û	*oo*	tion	*syōn* (see above)
ç	*s* (see above)	qu	*k*
au(x), eau(x)	*oh* (see above)	h	silent
eu(x), œ(u)	*uh* (see above)	ll	sometimes *y* (see above)
oi, oî, oy	*wa/wah*		

If you are travelling in Switzerland, remember that each canton has its own local holidays.

New Year's Day	January 1st
Good Friday	*(Switzerland only)*
Easter Monday	
Labour Day	May 1st *(not Switzerland)*
Ascension Day	
Whit Monday	
Bastille Day	July 14th *(France only)*
National Holiday	July 21st *(Belgium only)*
Assumption	August 15th *(not Switzerland)*
All Saints' Day	November 1st *(not Switzerland)*
Armistice Day	November 11th *(not Switzerland)*
Christmas Day	December 25th
St Stephen's Day	December 26th *(not France)*

See also LUGGAGE, TRAIN TRAVEL

Children under ten pay half fare and those under four travel
free. At the platform entrance the sign "N'oubliez pas de
composter votre billet" indicates the automatic machine into
which tickets should be inserted for date-stamping.

What time are the trains to ...? A quelle
heure sont les trains pour ...?
a kel ur soñ lay trañ poor ...

When is the next train to ...? A quelle
heure est le prochain train pour ...?
a kel ur eh luh proshañ trañ poor ...

What time does it get there? Il arrive à
quelle heure?
eel areev a kel ur

Do I have to change? Est-ce que je dois
changer?
es kuh zhuh dwah shoñ-zhay

A return/single to ..., first/second class
Un aller-retour/Un aller simple pour
..., en première/seconde classe
*uñn alay-ruhtoor/uñn alay sañpl poor ...
oñ pruh-myehr/suhgoñd klas*

**I want to book a seat in a non-smoking
compartment** Je voudrais réserver une
place dans un compartiment non-
fumeur
*zhuh voodray rayzehr-vay oon plas doñz
uñ koñpar-teemoñ noñ-foomur*

I want to reserve a couchette/sleeper Je
voudrais réserver une couchette/une
place de wagon-lit
*zhuh voodray rayzehr-vay oon
kooshet/oon plas duh vagoñ-lee*

Which platform for the train to ...? Pour
..., c'est quel quai?
poor ... seh kel kay

arrival
l'arrivée
aree-vay
buffet
le buffet
boofay
departure
le départ
daypar
guard
le chef de train
shef duh trañ
half fare
le demi-tarif
duhmee-tareef
left luggage
la consigne
koñsee-nyuh
reservation
la réservation
rayzehr-va-syoñ
supplement
le supplément
sooplay-moñ
ticket office
le guichet
geesheh
timetable board
le tableau des
horaires
tabloh dayz orehr
waiting room
la salle d'attente
sal datoñt

See also ACCIDENTS, BREAKDOWNS, EMERGENCIES

I have broken the window J'ai cassé la fenêtre
zhay kassay la fuhnetr

There is a hole in these trousers Il y a un trou dans ce pantalon
eel ya uñ troo doñ suh poñta-loñ

This is broken/torn C'est cassé/déchiré
seh kassay / dayshee-ray

Can you repair this? Pouvez-vous réparer ça?
poovay-voo raypa-ray sa

Can you do it quickly? Pouvez-vous le réparer rapidement?
poovay-voo luh raypa-ray rapeed-moñ

When can you get it done by? Vous pouvez le faire pour quand?
voo poovay luh fehr poor koñ

I need some glue/a safety pin J'ai besoin de colle/d'une épingle de sûreté
zhay buhzwañ duh kol / doon aypañ-gluh duh soortay

The stitching has come undone Les piqûres se sont défaites
lay peekoor suh soñ dayfet

Can you reheel these shoes? Pouvez-vous remettre un talon à ces chaussures?
poovay-voo ruhmetr uñ taloñ a say shohsoor

The screw has come loose La vis s'est défaite
la vees seh dayfet

The handle has come off La poignée s'est détachée
la pwah-nyay seh dayta-shay

button le bouton
bootoñ

glue la colle
kol

hammer le marteau
martoh

nail le clou
kloo

pin une épingle
aypañ-gluh

screwdriver le tournevis
toorn-vees

string la ficelle
feesel

tape le ruban
rooboñ

temporary provisoire
proveez-wahr

See also DRIVING ABROAD, ROAD SIGNS, WEATHER

Minor roads signposted with green arrows (*flèches vertes*)
   offer excellent alternative routes when traffic reaches its peak
   during the summer. In snowy weather studded snow tyres or
   chains may be compulsory.

Is there a route that avoids the traffic?
   Est-ce qu'il y a un itinéraire qui évite
   les encombrements?
   *es keel ya uñn eetee-nayrehr kee ayveet
   layz oñkoñ-bruhmoñ*

Is the traffic heavy on the motorway?
   Est-ce qu'il y a beaucoup de circulation
   sur l'autoroute?
   *es keel ya bohkoo duh seerkoo-la-syoñ
   soor lohtoh-root*

What is causing this hold-up? Quelle est
   la cause de ce bouchon?
   kel eh la kohz duh suh booshoñ

When will the road be clear? La route
   sera dégagée dans combien de temps?
   *la root suhra dayga-zhay doñ koñ-byañ
   duh toñ*

Is there a detour? Est-ce qu'il y a une
   déviation?
   es keel ya oon day-vya-syoñ

Is the road to ... snowed up? Est-ce que
   la route de ... est enneigée?
   es kuh la root duh ... eh oñneh-zhay

Is the pass/tunnel open? Est-ce que le
   col/tunnel est ouvert?
   es kuh luh kol/toonel eh oovehr

Do I need chains/studded tyres? Est-ce
   que les chaînes/les pneus cloutés sont
   nécessaires?
   *es kuh lay shen/lay pnuh klootay soñ
   naysay-sehr*

accident
un accident
aksee-doñ
black ice
le verglas
vehrgla
fog
le brouillard
broo-yar
frost
le gel
zhel
rain
la pluie
plwee
road conditions
l'état des routes
ayta day root
road works
les travaux
travoh
tailback
le bouchon
booshoñ
traffic jam
un embouteillage
oñboo-tay-yazh

See also DRIVING ABROAD, NOTICES

Accès interdit
No entry

Accotements non stabilisés
Soft verge

Aire de repos
Lay-by

Allumez vos lanternes/phares
Switch on headlights

Attention! vous n'avez pas la priorité
Warning! give way to traffic from the right

Autoroute
Motorway

Autres directions
Other destinations

Cédez le passage
Give way

Centre-ville
City centre, town centre

Chantier
Roadworks

Chaussée déformée
Uneven road surface

Chaussée verglacée
Icy road surface, slippery road

Circuit touristique
Scenic route

Défense de stationner
No parking

Déviation
Diversion

Douane
Customs

Fin d'interdiction de stationner
End of parking restrictions

Interdit aux piétons
Pedestrians prohibited

Passage à niveau
Level crossing

Passage protégé
Priority road, You have priority

Péage
Toll

Poids lourds
Heavy goods vehicles

Priorité à droite
Give way to traffic coming from the right

Ralentir
Slow down

Rappel
Reminder

Route barrée
Road closed

Sans issue
No through road

Sens unique
One way

Serrez à droite
Keep right

Sortie de camions
Lorries crossing

Sortie de secours
Emergency exit

Stationnement interdit
No parking

Toutes directions
Through traffic

Travaux
Road works

Virages sur 2 km
Bends for 2 km

Vitesse limitée à ...
Speed limit ...

Zone piétonnière
Pedestrian precinct

See also CLEANING, COMPLAINTS, HOTEL DESK, TELEPHONE

Come in! Entrez!
ōntray

We'd like breakfast/a bottle of wine in our room Nous voudrions le petit déjeuner/une bouteille de vin dans notre chambre
noo voodree-ōñ luh puhtee day-zhuh-nay / oon bootay duh vāñ dōñ notr shōñbr

Put it on my bill Mettez-le sur ma note
metay-luh soor ma not

I'd like an outside line please C'est pour une communication extérieure
seh poor oon komoo-neeka-syōñ ekstay-ryur

I have lost my key J'ai perdu ma clé
zhay pehrdoo ma klay

I have locked myself out of my room Je me suis enfermé dehors
zhuh muh swee ōñfehr-may duh-or

Where is the socket for my electric razor? Où est la prise de courant pour mon rasoir électrique?
oo eh la preez duh koorōñ poor mōñ razwahr aylek-treek

What's the voltage? Quel est le voltage?
kel eh luh voltazh

I need a hairdryer/an iron J'ai besoin d'un sèche-cheveux/d'un fer à repasser
zhay buhzwāñ dūñ sesh-shuhvuh / dūñ fehr a ruh-passay

May I have an extra blanket/pillow? Est-ce que je peux avoir une couverture/un oreiller supplémentaire?
es kuh zhuh puh avwahr oon koovehr-toor / ūñ oray-yay sooplay-mōñtehr

The TV/radio does not work La télé/radio ne marche pas
la taylay / ra-dyoh nuh marsh pa

Please send someone to collect my luggage Vous voulez bien envoyer quelqu'un pour prendre mes bagages
voo voolay byāñ ōñvwa-yay kelkūñ poor prōñdr may bagazh

We are going aboard now Nous allons embarquer
nooz alōn ōnbar-kay

The wind is getting up Le vent se lève
luh vōn suh lev

It's blowing hard from the north Le vent souffle très fort du nord
luh vōn soofluh treh for doo nor

It's flat calm C'est le calme plat
seh luh kalm pla

Ready about! Pare à virer!
par a veeray

Hard to port/starboard A bâbord/tribord toute
a babor / treebor toot

We'll have to use the engine Il faut utiliser le moteur
eel foh ootee-leezay luh motur

When is the weather forecast? A quelle heure est la météo?
a kel ur eh la maytay-oh

We'll anchor here for the night Nous jetterons l'ancre ici pour la nuit
noo zhetrōn lōnkr eesee poor la nwee

Please take my mooring line Prenez l'amarre
pruhnay lamar

I'm feeling seasick J'ai le mal de mer
zhay luh mal duh mehr

anchor
une ancre
ōnkr

boom
la bôme
bohm

bow
l'avant
avōn

dinghy
le youyou
yoo-yoo

harbour
le port
por

jib
le foc
fok

mast
le mât
mah

propeller
une hélice
aylees

rudder
le gouvernail
goovehr-nye

sail
la voile
vwahl

sheet
une écoute
aykoot

stern
l'arrière
a-ryehr

We've booked an apartment in the name of ... Nous avons réservé un appartement au nom de ...
nooz avôn rayzehr-vay ũnn apar-tuhmôn oh nôn duh ...

Which is the key for the front door? Quelle est la clé de la porte d'entrée?
kel eh la klay duh la port dôntray

Please show us around Est-ce que vous pourriez nous faire visiter?
es kuh voo pooree-ay noo fehr veezee-tay

Where is the electricity meter? Où se trouve le compteur électrique?
oo suh troov luh kôntur aylek-treek

How does the heating/the shower work? Le chauffage/La douche marche comment?
luh shohfazh/la doosh marsh komôn

When does the cleaner come? La femme de ménage vient quand?
la fam duh maynazh vyãn kôn

Is the cost of electricity included in the rental? Est-ce que l'électricité est comprise dans la location?
es kuh laylek-treesee-tay eh kônpreez dôn la loka-syôn

Is there any extra bedding? Est-ce qu'il y a des couvertures supplémentaires?
es keel ya day koovehr-toor sooplay-môntehr

A fuse has blown Les plombs ont sauté
lay plôn ôn sohtay

Where can I contact you? Où est-ce que je peux vous contacter?
oo es kuh zhuh puh voo kôntak tay

bathroom
la salle de bains
sal duh bãn
bedroom
la chambre à coucher
shônbr a kooshay
cooker
la cuisinière
kweezee-nyehr
fridge
le frigo
freegoh
gas
le gaz
gaz
heater
un appareil de chauffage
apa-ray duh shohfazh
kitchen
la cuisine
kweezeen
light
la lumière
loo-myehr
living room
la salle de séjour
sal duh say-zhoor
sheet
le drap
dra
toilet
les toilettes
twalet
water heater
le chauffe-eau
shohf-oh

See also BUYING, PAYING

Where is the main shopping area? Où se
trouvent la plupart des magasins?
oo suh troov la ploopar day maga-zañ

Where are the big stores? Où sont les
grands magasins?
oo soñ lay groñ maga-zañ

What time do the shops close? Les
magasins ferment à quelle heure?
lay maga-zañ fehrm a kel ur

How much is that? Ça coûte combien?
sa koot koñ-byañ

How much is it per kilo/per metre? Ça
fait combien le kilo/le mètre?
sa feh koñ-byañ luh keeloh / luh metr

Can I try it on? Est-ce que je peux
l'essayer?
es kuh zhuh puh lessay-yay

Where is the shoe/food department? Où
est le rayon des chaussures/
d'alimentation?
oo eh luh ray-yoñ day shohsoor / dalee-moñta-syoñ

I'm looking for a gift for my wife Je
cherche un cadeau pour ma femme
zhuh shersh uñ kadoh poor ma fam

I'm just looking Je regarde seulement
zhuh ruhgard suhlmoñ

**Have you anything suitable for a small
boy?** Est-ce que vous avez quelque
chose pour un petit garçon?
*es kuh vooz avay kelkuh shohz poor uñ
puhtee garsoñ*

Can I have a carrier bag please? Puis-je
avoir un sac en plastique?
pweezh avwahr uñ sak oñ plasteek

cash desk
la caisse
kes

changing room
le salon
d'essayage
saloñ dessay-yazh

closed
fermé
fehrmay

exit
la sortie
sortee

market
le marché
marshay

open
ouvert
oovehr

paper bag
le sac en papier
sak oñ pa-pyay

shopping bag
le sac (à
provisions)
sak (a provee-syoñ)

stall
le kiosque
kee-osk

window
la vitrine
veetreen

See also MAPS AND GUIDES, TRIPS AND EXCURSIONS

For general information go to the local Tourist Information
Office - *le syndicat d'initiative* (*sañdee-ka deenee-sya-teev*).

What is there to see here? Qu'est-ce qu'il y a à voir dans la région? *kes keel ya a vwahr dōñ la ray-zhyoñ*	**guide book** le guide *geed*
Excuse me, how do I get to the cathedral? Pardon, pour la cathédrale s'il vous plaît *pardōñ poor la katay-dral seel voo pleh*	**map** la carte *kart*
Where is the museum/the main square? Le musée/La place centrale, s'il vous plaît *luh moozay/la plas sōñtral seel voo pleh*	**park** le jardin public *zhardāñ poobleek* **souvenirs** les souvenirs *soov-neer*
What time does the guided tour begin? La visite guidée commence à quelle heure? *la veezeet geeday komōñs a kel ur*	**street plan** le plan des rues *plōñ day roo*
What time does the museum open? Le musée ouvre à quelle heure? *luh moozay oovr a kel ur*	**trip** une excursion *ekskoor-syōñ* **view** la vue *voo*
Is the castle open to the public? Est-ce que le château est ouvert au public? *es kuh luh shatoh eh oovehr oh poobleek*	
How much does it cost to get in? L'entrée coûte combien? *lōñtray koot kōñbyāñ*	
Can we take photographs in here? C'est permis de prendre des photos? *seh pehrmee duh prōñdr day fohtoh*	
Where can I buy a film/some ice cream? Où est-ce que je peux acheter un film/des glaces? *oo es kuh zhuh puh ashtay ūñ feelm/day glas*	

The simplest way to buy tobacco is from a *café-tabac* (*kafay-taba*), i.e. a café with a red "TABAC" sign outside. Smoking is not permitted on the *métro*. Keep a look-out for the "No Smoking" sign - *Défense de fumer* - when in public places or travelling by public transport.

Do you mind if I smoke? Ça vous dérange si je fume?
sa voo dayrōñzh see zhuh foom

May I have an ashtray? Un cendrier, s'il vous plaît
uñ sōñdree-ay seel voo pleh

Is this a no-smoking compartment/area? Est-ce que c'est un compartiment/une zone non-fumeur?
es kuh seh uñ kōñpar-teemōñ / oon zon nōñ-foomur

A packet of ... please Un paquet de ..., s'il vous plaît
uñ pakeh duh ... seel voo pleh

Have you got any American/English cigarettes? Est-ce que vous avez des cigarettes américaines/anglaises?
es kuh vooz avay day seega-ret amay-reeken / ōñglez

I'd like some pipe tobacco Du tabac pour la pipe, s'il vous plaît
doo taba poor la peep seel voo pleh

Do you have any matches/pipe cleaners? Avez-vous des allumettes/des cure-pipes?
avay-voo dayz aloo-met / day koor-peep

Have you a refill for my lighter? Avez-vous une recharge pour mon briquet?
avay-voo oon ruhsharzh poor mōñ breekeh

Have you got a light? Avez-vous du feu?
avay-voo doo fuh

box of matches la boîte d'allumettes
bwaht daloo-met

brand la marque
mark

cigar le cigare
seegar

cigarette papers les papiers à cigarettes
pa-pyay a seega-ret

filter le filtre
feeltr

filter-tipped à bout filtre
a boo feeltr

pipe la pipe
peep

See also BEACH, ENTERTAINMENT, SAILING, WATERSPORTS,
WINTER SPORTS

Which sports activities are available here? On peut pratiquer quels sports, ici?
oñ puh pratee-kay kel spor eesee

Is it possible to go riding? Est-ce qu'on peut faire du cheval?
es koñ puh fehr doo shuhval

Where can we play tennis/golf? Où est-ce qu'on peut jouer au tennis/golf?
oo es koñ puh zhoo-ay oh tenees/golf

Is there a swimming pool? Est-ce qu'il y a une piscine?
es keel ya oon peeseen

Are there any interesting walks nearby? Est-ce qu'il y a de belles promenades à faire près d'ici?
es keel ya duh bel prom-nad a fehr preh deesee

Can we rent the equipment? Est-ce qu'on peut louer l'équipement?
es koñ puh loo-ay laykeep-moñ

How much does it cost per hour? C'est combien l'heure?
seh koñ-byañ lur

Do we need to be members? Est-ce qu'il faut être membre?
es keel foh etr moñbr

Where do we buy our tickets? Où est-ce qu'on achète les billets?
oo es koñ a-shet lay bee-yay

Can we take lessons? Est-ce qu'on peut prendre des leçons?
es koñ puh proñdr day luhsoñ

ball	la balle *bal*
climbing	l'escalade *eska-lad*
cycling	le cyclisme *seeklees-muh*
fishing	la pêche *pesh*
gym shoes	les tennis *tenees*
gymnasium	le gymnase *zheemnaz*
hill-walking	la randonnée en montagne *roñdo-nay oñ moñta-nyuh*
racket	la raquette *raket*
shorts	le short *short*
squash	le squash *skwosh*
swimming	la natation *nata-syoñ*

adhesive tape
le ruban adhésif
roobõn aday-zeef

biro
le stylo à bille
steeloh a beey

birthday card
la carte
d'anniversaire
kart danee-vehrsehr

book
le livre
leevr

cartridge.
la cartouche
kartoosh

coloured pencils
les crayons de
couleur
kray-yõn duh koolur

crayons
les pastels
pastel

drawing book
le bloc à dessin
blok a dessãn

envelopes
les enveloppes
õnvuh-lop

felt-tip pen
le stylo-feutre
steeloh-fuhtr

glue
la colle
kol

ink
l'encre
õnkr

luggage tag
une étiquette à
bagages
*aytee-ket a
bagazh*

magazine
la revue
ruhvoo

newspaper
le journal
zhoornal

note pad
le bloc-notes
blok-not

painting book
le carnet à
peinture
karneh a pãntoor

paints
la boîte de
couleurs
bwaht duh koolur

paper
le papier
pa-pyay

paperback
le livre de poche
leevr duh posh

paperclip
le trombone
trõnbon

pen
le stylo
steeloh

pencil
le crayon
kray-yõn

pencil sharpener
le taille-crayon
tye-kray-yõn

postcard
la carte postale
kart pos-tal

refill (for biro)
la recharge
ruhsharzh

rubber
la gomme
gom

stapler
une agrafeuse
agra-fuhz

staples
les agrafes
agraf

writing paper
le papier à lettres
pa-pyay a letr

You can phone for a taxi, or hail one provided you are not
within 50 metres of a taxi rank. Tip: 15% to 20%.

Can you order me a taxi please? Pouvez-vous m'appeler un
taxi, s'il vous plaît?
poovay-voo maplay uñ taxi seel voo pleh

To the main station/airport please A la gare/A l'aéroport, s'il
vous plaît
a la gar / a la-ehro-por seel voo pleh

Take me to this address/hotel A cette adresse/cet hôtel, s'il
vous plaît
a set a-dress / set ohtel seel voo pleh

Is it far? Est-ce que c'est loin?
es kuh seh lwañ

How much will it cost? Ça va faire combien?
sa va fehr koñ-byañ

I'm in a hurry Je suis pressé
zhuh swee pressay

Can you wait here for a few minutes? Est-ce que vous pouvez
m'attendre ici quelques instants?
es kuh voo poovay ma-toñdr eesee kelkuhz añstoñ

Turn left/right here Tournez à gauche/à droite ici
toornay a gohsh / a drwaht eesee

Please stop here/at the corner Arrêtez-vous ici/au coin
areh-tay-voo eesee / oh kwañ

How much is it? Ça fait combien?
sa feh koñ-byañ

It's more than on the meter C'est plus cher que sur le
compteur
seh ploo shehr kuh soor luh koñtur

Keep the change Gardez la monnaie
garday la monay

Make it (20 francs etc) Rendez-moi sur (20 francs etc)
roñday-mwah soor ...

Can you give me a receipt? Pouvez-vous me donner un reçu?
poovay-voo muh donay uñ ruhsoo

Most phones take 50c, 1F, 2F and 5F coins, although some older phones in cafés require tokens (*jetons: zhuhtōn*) bought at the bar. In phone booths the money is inserted before dialling, coins being refunded if you hang up without getting through. For international calls dial 19 followed by your country code (44 for Britain).

Can I have a line to ...? Je voudrais appeler ...
zhuh voodray aplay ...

I want to make a phone call Je voudrais téléphoner
zhuh voodray taylay-fonay

The number is ... C'est le numéro ...
seh luh noomay-roh ...

I want to reverse the charges Je voudrais téléphoner en P.C.V.
zhuh voodray taylay-fonay ōn pay-say-vay

Have you got change for the phone? Avez-vous de la monnaie pour le téléphone?
avay-voo duh la monay poor luh taylay-fon

What coins do I need? J'ai besoin de quelles pièces?
zhay buhzwañ duh kel pyess

How much is it to phone Britain? Ça coûte combien pour téléphoner en Grande-Bretagne?
sa koot kōñ-byañ poor taylay-fonay ōn grōñd-bruhta-nyuh

I can't get through Je n'arrive pas à obtenir la communication
zhuh nareev pa a optuh-neer la komoo-neeka-syōñ

The line's engaged C'est occupé
seh okoo-pay

dialling code
l'indicatif
añdee-kateef

dialling tone
la tonalité
tona-leetay

directory
un annuaire
anoo-ehr

extension
le poste
post

operator
le/la téléphoniste
taylay-foneest

phone box
la cabine téléphonique
kabeen taylay-foneek

receiver
le récepteur
raysep-tur

transfer charge call
un appel en P.C.V.
apel ōñ pay-say-vay

Hello, this is ... Allô, ... à l'appareil
alo ... a lapa-ray

Can I speak to Jean Dubois? Est-ce que je peux parler à Jean Dubois?
es kuh zhuh puh parlay a ...

I've been cut off Nous avons été coupés
nooz avoñ aytay koopay

It's a bad line La ligne est mauvaise
la lee-nyuh eh movez

YOU MAY HEAR:

Ne quittez pas!
nuh keetay pa
I'm trying to connect you/Hold the line

Je vous le passe
zhuh voo luh pas
I'm putting you through

Je suis désolé mais la ligne est occupée
zhuh swee dayzoh-lay meh la lee-nyuh eh okoo-pay
I'm sorry, it's engaged

Est-ce que vous pouvez rappeler plus tard?
es kuh voo poovay raplay ploo tar
Can you try again later?

C'est de la part de qui?
seh duh la par duh kee
Who's calling?

Ce n'est pas le bon numéro
suh neh pa luh boñ noomay-roh
Sorry, wrong number

See also NUMBERS

What's the time?	**It's:**
Quelle heure est-il?	Il est:
Kel ur eteel	*eel eh*

8.00	huit heures
	weet ur
8.05	huit heures cinq
	weet ur sānk
8.10	huit heures dix
	weet ur dees
8.15	huit heures et quart
	weet ur ay kar
8.20	huit heures vingt
	weet ur vān
8.25	huit heures vingt-cinq
	weet ur vān-sānk
8.30	huit heures et demie
	weet ur ay duhmee
8.35	neuf heures moins vingt-cinq
	nuhv ur mwān vān-sānk
8.40	neuf heures moins vingt
	nuhv ur mwān vān
8.45	neuf heures moins le quart
	nuhv ur mwān luh kar
8.50	neuf heures moins dix
	nuhv ur mwān dees
8.55	neuf heures moins cinq
	nuhv ur mwān sānk
12.00	midi (*midday*); minuit (*midnight*)
	meedee *meenwee*

You may hear the 24-hour clock:

9.00pm	**21.00**	vingt et une heures
		vānt ay oon ur
4.45pm	**16.45**	seize heures quarante-cinq
		sez ur karōnt-sānk

What time do you open/close? Vous ouvrez/Vous fermez à
quelle heure?
vooz oovray / voo fehrmay a kel ur

Do we have time to visit the town? Est-ce que nous avons le
temps de visiter la ville?
es kuh nooz avōñ luh tōñ duh veezee-tay la veel

How long will it take to get there? Combien de temps faut-il
pour y aller?
kōñ-byañ duh tōñ foht-eel poor ee alay

We can be there in half an hour On peut y être dans une demi-
heure
ōñ puh ee etr dōñz oon duhmee-ur

We arrived early/late Nous sommes arrivés en avance/en retard
noo som aree-vay ōñn avōñs / ōñ ruhtar

We should have been there two hours ago On aurait dû y être
il y a deux heures
ōñ oray doo ee etr eel ya duhz ur

We must be back at the hotel before 11 o'clock Il faut être de
retour à l'hôtel avant onze heures
eel foh etr duh ruhtoor a lohtel avōñ ōñz ur

When does the coach leave in the morning? Le car part à
quelle heure le matin?
luh kar par a kel ur luh matañ

The tour starts at about half past three La visite guidée
commence vers trois heures et demie
la veezeet geeday komōñs vehr trwahz ur ay duhmee

The museum is open in the morning/afternoon Le musée est
ouvert le matin/l'après-midi
luh moozay eh oovehr luh matañ / lapreh-meedee

The table is booked for 8.30 this evening On a réservé une
table pour huit heures et demie ce soir
ōñ a rayzehr-vay oon tabluh poor weet ur ay duhmee suh swahr

See also TAXIS, TOILETS

Most cafés and restaurants include the service charge in the bill, itemised as *Service Compris* with the relevant percentage shown. If the service charge is not included - *Service Non Compris* - you should add between 12½ and 15 percent. Small coins given in the change are usually left for the waiter, in any event. Hotel staff (such as the chambermaid and the porter) should also receive a small gratuity. Museum attendants or guides should be given 1F - 2F, and cinema usherettes 2F.

Sorry, I don't have any change Je regrette, mais je n'ai pas de monnaie
zhuh ruhgret meh zhuh nay pa duh monay

Could you give me change of ...? Pourriez-vous me faire la monnaie de ...?
pooree-ay-voo muh fehr la monay duh ...

Is it usual to tip ...? Est-ce qu'on donne habituellement un pourboire à ...?
es kōñ don abee-too-elmōñ uñ poorbwahr a ...

How much should I tip? Je devrais donner un pourboire de combien?
zhuh duhvray donay uñ poorbwahr duh kōñ-byañ

Is the tip included? Est-ce que le service est compris?
es kuh luh sehrvees eh kōñpree

Keep the change Gardez la monnaie
garday la monay

aftershave
la lotion après-rasage
loh-syōn aàpreh-razazh

baby wipes
les serviettes rafraîchissantes
sehr-vyet rafreh-sheesōnt

blusher
le rouge à joues
roozh a zhoo

cleansing cream
la crème démaquillante
krem dayma-kee-yōnt

cotton wool
la ouate
wat

deodorant
le déodorant
dayoh-dorōn

eye liner
l'eye-liner
eye-liner

eye shadow
l'ombre à paupières
ōnbr a poh-pyehr

eyebrow pencil
le crayon à sourcils
kray-yōn a soorseey

face cloth
le gant de toilette
gōn duh twalet

face powder
la poudre de riz
poodr duh ree

hand cream
la crème pour les mains
krem poor lay mān

lipstick
le rouge à lèvres
roozh a levr

mascara
le mascara
maska-ra

moisturizer
le lait hydratant
leh eedra-tōn

nail file
la lime à ongles
leem a ōngluh

nail polish
le vernis à ongles
vehrnee a ōngluh

nail polish remover
le dissolvant
deesol-vōn

paper handkerchiefs
les mouchoirs en papier
mooshwahr ōn pa-pyay

perfume
le parfum
parfūn

razor
le rasoir
razwahr

razor blades
les lames de rasoir
lam duh razwahr

shampoo
le shampooing
shōnpwān

shaving cream
la crème à raser
krem a razay

soap
le savon
savōn

sponge
une éponge
aypōnzh

sponge bag
le sac de toilette
sak duh twalet

sun-tan cream
la crème solaire
krem solehr

talc
le talc
talk

tissues
les kleenex
kleenex

toilet water
l'eau de toilette
oh duh twalet

toothbrush
la brosse à dents
bros a dōn

toothpaste
le dentifrice
dōntee-frees

Lavatory attendants are customarily given a tip of not less than 50 centimes.

Where are the toilets, please? Les toilettes, s'il vous plaît
lay twalet seel voo pleh

Do you have to pay? Est-ce qu'il faut payer?
es keel foh pay-yay

This toilet does not flush La chasse d'eau ne marche pas
la shas doh nuh marsh pa

There is no toilet paper/soap Il n'y a pas de papier hygiénique/de savon
eel nya pa duh pa-pyay ee-zhyay-neek / duh savoñ

Is there a toilet for the disabled? Est-ce qu'il y a des toilettes pour handicapés?
es keel ya day twalet poor oñdee-kapay

Are there facilities for mothers with babies? Est-ce qu'il y a un endroit pour changer les bébés?
es keel ya uñn oñdrwah poor shoñ-zhay lay baybay

The towels have run out Les essuie-mains sont finis
layz eswee-mañ soñ feenee

The door will not close La porte ne ferme pas
la port nuh fehrm pa

attendant
le gardien
gar-dyañ

contraceptives
les contraceptifs
koñtra-septeef

mirror
la glace
glas

sanitary towels
les serviettes hygiéniques
sehr-vyet ee-zhyay-neek

seat
le siège
syezh

tampons
les tampons
toñpoñ

vending machine
le distributeur automatique
deestree-bootur ohtoh-mateek

washbasin
le lavabo
lava-boh

waste bin
la poubelle
poobel

See also LUGGAGE, RAILWAY STATION, TRAVEL AGENT

Is this the train for ...? Est-ce que c'est
le train pour ...?
es kuh seh luh trañ poor ...

Is this seat free? Est-ce que cette place
est libre?
es kuh set plas eh leebr

**Can you help me put my suitcase in the
luggage rack?** Pouvez-vous m'aider à
mettre ma valise sur le porte-bagages?
*poovay-voo meday a metr ma valeez
soor luh port-bagazh*

May I open the window? Est-ce que je
peux ouvrir la fenêtre?
es kuh zhuh puh oovreer la fuhnetr

What time do we get to ...? Nous
arrivons à quelle heure à ...?
nooz aree-voñ a kel ur a ...

Do we stop at ...? Est-ce que le train
s'arrête à ...?
es kuh luh trañ saret a ...

Where do I change for ...? Où est-ce que
je change pour aller à ...?
oo es kuh zhuh shoñzh poor alay a ...

Is there a buffet car/restaurant car? Est-
ce qu'il y a un buffet/wagon-
restaurant?
es keel ya uñ boofay / vagoñ-resto-roñ

This is a no-smoking compartment Ici,
c'est un compartiment non-fumeur
eesee seh uñ koñpar-teemoñ noñ-foomur

Please tell me when we get to ... Dites-
moi, s'il vous plaît, lorsque nous serons
à ...
*deet-mwah seel voo pleh lorskuh noo
suhroñ a ...*

alarm
l'alarme
alarm

compartment
le compartiment
koñpar-teemoñ

corridor
le couloir
koolwahr

couchette
la couchette
kooshet

driver
le conducteur
koñdook-tur

express
le rapide
rapeed

guard
le chef de train
shef duh trañ

sleeping car
la voiture-lit
vwatoor-lee

stopping train
un omnibus
omnee-boos

ticket collector
le contrôleur
koñtroh-lur

toilet
les toilettes
twalet

What's the best way to get to ...? Quelle est la meilleure façon
pour aller à ...?
kel eh la may-yur fasoñ poor alay a ...

How much is it to fly to ...? Ça coûte combien pour aller en
avion à ...?
sa koot koñ-byañ poor alay oñn a-vyoñ a ...

Are there any special cheap fares? Est-ce qu'il existe des tarifs
réduits spéciaux?
es keel egzeest day tareef raydwee spay-syoh

What times are the trains/flights? Quel est l'horaire des
trains/vols?
kel eh lorehr day trañ/vol

Can I buy the tickets here? Est-ce que je peux acheter les
billets ici?
es kuh zhuh puh ashtay lay bee-yay eesee

Can I change my booking? Est-ce que je peux changer ma
réservation?
es kuh zhuh puh shoñ-zhay ma rayzehr-va-syoñ

Can you book me on the London flight? Pouvez-vous me
réserver une place sur le vol de Londres?
poovay-voo muh rayzehr-vay oon plas soor luh vol duh loñdr

Can I get back to Manchester tonight? Est-ce que je peux
rentrer à Manchester ce soir?
es kuh zhuh puh roñtray a manchester suh swahr

Two second class returns to ... 2 aller-retour en deuxième
classe pour ...
duhz alay-ruhtoor oñ duh-zyem klas poor ...

Can you book me into a hotel? Pouvez-vous me réserver une
chambre dans un hôtel?
poovay-voo muh rayzehr-vay oon shoñbr doñz uññ ohtel

Do you do bookings for shows/concerts? Est-ce que vous faites
les réservations pour les spectacles/concerts?
es kuh voo fet lay rayzehr-va-syoñ poor lay spektakl/koñsehr

A ticket for tonight's performance Un billet pour la séance de
ce soir
uñ bee-yay poor la sayoñs duh suh swahr

See also SIGHTSEEING

Are there any sightseeing tours? Y a-t-il des excursions organisées?
ee ateel dayz ekskoor-syōn orga-neezay

When is the bus tour of the town? La visite guidée de la ville en bus est à quelle heure?
la veezeet geeday duh la veel ōn boos eh a kel ur

How long does the tour take? La visite dure combien de temps?
la veezeet door kōn-byān duh tōn

Are there any boat trips on the river/lake? Y a-t-il des excursions en bateau sur la rivière/le lac?
ee ateel dayz ekskoor-syōn ōn batoh soor la ree-vyehr/luh lak

Is there a guided tour of the cathedral? Est-ce qu'il y a une visite guidée de la cathédrale?
es keel ya oon veezeet geeday duh la katay-dral

Is there a reduction for children/senior citizens/a group? Y a-t-il une réduction pour les enfants/les retraités/un groupe?
ee ateel oon raydook-syōn poor layz ōnfōn/lay ruhtreh-tay/ūn groop

Is there a commentary in English? Est-ce qu'il y a un commentaire en anglais?
es keel ya ūn komōn-tehr ōnn ōngleh

Please stop the bus, my child is feeling sick! Arrêtez le bus, s'il vous plaît, mon enfant a mal au cœur!
areh-tay luh boos seel voo pleh mon ōnfōn a mal oh kur

coach trip une excursion en car *ekskoor-syōn ōn kar*
excursion une excursion *ekskoor-syōn*
fare le prix du billet *pree doo bee-yay*
organized organisé *orga-neezay*
party le groupe *groop*
ticket le billet *bee-yay*
tour une excursion *ekskoor-syōn*
visit la visite *veezeet*
zoo le zoo *zoh*

bottle opener
un ouvre-bouteilles
oovr-bootay

broom
le balai
balay

can opener
un ouvre-boîtes
oovr-bwaht

chair
la chaise
shez

cloth
la lavette
lavet

clothespeg
la pince à linge
pāns a lānzh

coat hanger
le cintre
sāntr

comb
le peigne
peh-nyuh

contact lenses
les verres de contact
vehr duh kōntakt

corkscrew
le tire-bouchon
teer-booshōn

cup
la tasse
tas

dish
le plat
pla

elastic band
un élastique
aylas-teek

flask
le thermos
tehrmos

fork
la fourchette
foorshet

frying-pan
la poêle
pwahl

glasses
les lunettes
loonet

hairbrush
la brosse à cheveux
bros a shuhvuh

hairgrip
la pince à cheveux
pāns a shuhvuh

handkerchief
le mouchoir
mooshwahr

knife
le couteau
kootoh

needle and thread
une aiguille et du fil
aygwee ay doo feel

penknife
le canif
kaneef

plate
une assiette
a-syet

plug
la prise
preez

rope
la corde
kord

safety pin
une épingle de sûreté
aypān-gluh duh soortay

saucepan
la casserole
kasrol

scissors
les ciseaux
seezoh

spoon
la cuiller
kwee-yehr

torch
la lampe de poche
lōnp duh posh

umbrella
le parapluie
para-plwee

vacuum cleaner
un aspirateur
aspee-ratur

washing-up liquid
le produit lave-vaisselle
prodwee lav-veh-sel

See also BEACH, SAILING

Is it possible to go water-skiing/wind-surfing? Est-il possible de faire du ski nautique/de la planche à voile?
ehteel poseebl duh fehr doo skee nohteek / duh la plõñsh a vwahl

Can we rent a motor boat/rowing boat? Est-ce qu'on peut louer un bateau à moteur/bateau à rames?
es kõñ puh loo-ay ũñ batoh a motur / batoh a ram

Can I rent a sailboard? Est-ce qu'on peut louer une planche à voile?
es kõñ puh loo-ay oon plõñsh a vwahl

Can one swim in the river? Peut-on se baigner dans la rivière?   –
puht-õñ suh bay-nyay dõñ la ree-vyehr

Can we fish here? Est-ce qu'on peut pêcher ici?
es kõñ puh payshay eesee

Is there a paddling pool for the children? Est-ce qu'il y a un petit bain pour les enfants?
es keel ya ũñ puhtee bãñ poor layz õñfõñ

Where is the municipal swimming pool? Où est la piscine municipale?
oo eh la peeseen moonee-seepal

Is the pool heated? Est-ce que la piscine est chauffée?
es kuh la peeseen eh shohfay

Is it an outdoor pool? Est-ce que c'est une piscine en pleine air?
es kuh seh oon peeseen õñ plen ehr

canoe
le canoë
kano-eh
flippers
les palmes
palm
goggles
les lunettes de plongée
loonet duh plõñ-zhay
life jacket
le gilet de sauve-tage
zheeleh duh sohvtazh
oar
la rame
ram
scuba-diving
la plongée sous-marine
plõñ-zhay soo-mareen
snorkel
le tuba
tooba
swimsuit
le maillot de bain
mye-yoh duh bãñ
wetsuit
la combinaison de plongée
kõñbee-nezõñ duh plõñ-zhay

It's a lovely day! Qu'il fait beau!
keel feh boh

What dreadful weather! Quel temps affreux!
kel tōn afruh

It is raining/snowing Il pleut/neige
eel pluh/nezh

It's windy/sunny/foggy Il fait du vent/du soleil/du brouillard
eel feh doo vōn/doo solay/doo broo-yar

There's a nice breeze blowing Il y a une petite brise agréable
eel ya oon puhteet breez agray-abl

Will it be cold tonight? Est-ce qu'il va faire froid cette nuit?
es keel va fehr frwah set nwee

Is it going to rain/to snow? Est-ce qu'il va pleuvoir/neiger?
es keel va pluhvwahr/neh-zhay

Will there be a frost? Est-ce qu'il va geler?
es keel va zhuh-lay

Will there be a thunderstorm? Est-ce qu'il va y avoir un orage?
es keel va ee avwahr ūnn orazh

Is it going to be fine? Est-ce qu'il va faire beau?
es keel va fehr boh

Is the weather going to change? Est-ce que le temps va changer?
es kuh luh tōn va shōn-zhay

What is the temperature? Quelle est la température?
kel eh la tōnpay-ratoor

calm	calme *kalm*
clouds	les nuages *noo-azh*
cool	frais *freh*
fog	le brouillard *broo-yar*
hot	très chaud *treh shoh*
mild	doux *doo*
mist	la brume *broom*
misty	brumeux *broomuh*
warm	chaud *shoh*
wet	pluvieux *ploo-vyuh*

We'd like an aperitif Un apéritif, s'il vous plaît
ūnn apay-reeteef seel voo pleh

May I have the wine list please? La carte des vins, s'il vous plaît
la kart day vãn seel voo pleh

Can you recommend a good red/white/rosé wine? Pouvez-vous nous conseiller un bon vin rouge/blanc/rosé?
poovay-voo noo kõnsay-yay ũn bõn vãn roozh/blõn/rohzay

A bottle/carafe of house wine Une bouteille/carafe de la réserve du patron
oon bootay/karaf duh la rayzehrv doo patrõn

A half bottle Une demi-bouteille
oon duhmee-bootay

Would you bring another glass please? Un autre verre, s'il vous plaît
ũhn ohtr vehr seel voo pleh

This wine is not chilled Ce vin n'est pas assez frais
suh vãn neh pa assay freh

What liqueurs do you have? Qu'est-ce que vous avez comme liqueurs?
kes kuh vooz avay kom leekur

I'll have a brandy/Scotch Un cognac/whisky, s'il vous plaît
ũn kõn-yak/weeskee seel voo pleh

A gin and tonic Un gin-tonic
ũn djeen-toneek

A Campari and soda Un campari soda
ũn kampa-ree soda

A Martini and lemonade Un martini avec de la limonade
ũn martee-nee avek duh la leemo-nad

champagne
le champagne
shõnpa-nyuh

dry
sec
sek

medium
demi-sec
duhmee-sek

port
le porto
portoh

sherry
le sherry
shehree

sparkling
mousseux
moosuh

sweet
doux
doo

vermouth
le vermouth
vehrmoot

vodka
la vodka
vodka

See also EATING OUT, WINES AND SPIRITS

Alsace Region producing dry, German-type white wines
Barsac Sweet white wine (*Bordeaux*)
Beaujolais Light, fruity wines to be drunk young (*Burgundy*)
Bergerac Red and white wines (*Dordogne*)
Blanc de Blancs Any white wine made from white grapes only
Blanquette de Limoux Dry, sparkling white wine (*South West*)
Bordeaux Region producing red (claret), dry and sweet whites
Bourgogne Burgundy; region producing red and white wine
Bourgueuil Light, fruity red to be drunk young (*Loire*)
Chablis Dry, full-bodied white wine (*Burgundy*)
Chambertin Full-bodied red wine (*Burgundy*)
Champagne Sparkling white/rosé (*Champagne* appellation only)
Châteauneuf du Pape Full-bodied red wine (*Rhône*)
Côtes de Beaune Full-bodied red (*Burgundy*)
Côtes du Rhône Full-bodied red (*Rhône*)
Côtes du Roussillon Good ordinary red (*South*)
Gewürztraminer Fruity, spicy, white wine (*Alsace*)
Mâcon Good ordinary red and white wines (*Burgundy*)
Médoc Principal red wine area of *Bordeaux*
Meursault Dry white wine (*Burgundy*)
Monbazillac Sweet white and ordinary red wines (*Dordogne*)
Muscadet Very dry white wine (*Loire*)
Pouilly-Fuissé Light dry white wine (*Burgundy*)
Pouilly-Fumé Spicy, dry white wine (*Loire*)
Rosé d'Anjou Light, fruity rosé (*Loire*)
Saint-Emilion Good full-bodied red wine (*Bordeaux*)
Sancerre Dry white wine (*Loire*)
Sauternes Sweet white wine (*Bordeaux*)
Sylvaner Dry white wine (*Alsace*)
Vouvray Dry, sweet and sparkling white wines (*Loire*)

Vin blanc/rouge White/red wine
Vin en carafe/en pichet House wine served in a carafe/jug
Vin du pays Local wine
Vin ordinaire/de table Ordinary/table wine

Can we hire skis here? Est-ce qu'on peut louer des skis ici?
es kôñ puh loo-ay day skee eesee

Could you adjust my bindings? Pouvez-vous ajuster mes fixations?
poovay-voo a-zhoostay may feeksa-syôñ

A 3-day ticket please Une carte de 3 jours, s'il vous plaît
oon kart duh trwah zhoor seel voo pleh

What are the snow conditions? Quelles sont les conditions d'enneigement?
kel sôñ lay kôñdee-syôñ dôññezh-môñ

Is there a restaurant at the top station? Y a-t-il un restaurant à la gare supérieure?
ee ateel ûñ resto-rôñ a la gar soopay-ryur

Which are the easiest runs? Quelles sont les pistes les plus faciles?
kel sôñ lay peest lay ploo faseel

We'll take the gondola Nous prendrons le télécabine
noo prôñdrôñ luh taylay-kabeen

When is the last ascent? A quelle heure part la dernière benne?
a kel ur par la dehr-nyehr ben

Is there a danger of avalanches? Y a-t-il risque d'avalanche?
ee ateel reesk dava-lôñsh

The snow is very icy/heavy La neige est très glacée/lourde
la nezh eh treh glasay / loord

Where can we go skating? Où est-ce qu'on peut faire du patin?
oo es kôñ puh fehr doo patâñ

Is there a toboggan run? Y a-t-il une piste de luge?
ee ateel oon peest duh loozh

cablecar
le téléphérique
taylay-fayreek

chairlift
le télésiège
taylay-syezh

goggles
les lunettes protectrices
loonet protek-trees

instructor
le moniteur
monee-tur

lift
le téléski
taylay-skee

lift pass
un abonnement aux remontées
abon-môñ oh ruhmôñ-tay

rink
la patinoire
patee-nwahr

skates
les patins
patâñ

ski boot
la chaussure de ski
shohsoor duh skee

ski pole
le bâton (de ski)
bahtôñ (duh skee)

ski suit
la combinaison de ski
kôñbee-nezôñ duh skee

The following is a list of all the key words used in this book, with a cross reference to the topic(s) under which they appear. If you don't find the word you are looking for in the wordlist on any given page — look through the phrases.

aboard → SAILING
accelerator → CAR PARTS
accident → ACCIDENTS
account → MONEY
address → PERSONAL DETAILS
adhesive tape → REPAIRS, STATIONERY
admission charge → ENTERTAINMENT
adult → FERRIES
advance, in a. → LUGGAGE, PAYING
afternoon → TIME PHRASES
aftershave → TOILETRIES
air line → PETROL STATION
air mail → POST OFFICE
air-mattress → CAMPING AND CARAVANNING
airport → AIRPORT
alarm → TRAIN TRAVEL
alcohol → CUSTOMS AND PASSPORTS
allowance → CUSTOMS AND PASSPORTS
altar → CHURCH AND WORSHIP
alternator → CAR PARTS
ambulance → ACCIDENTS – INJURIES, EMERGENCIES
America → POST OFFICE
American → SMOKING
anchor → SAILING
ankle → BODY
antiseptic → CHEMIST'S
apartment → SELF-CATERING

aperitif → WINES AND SPIRITS
apples → FOOD – FRUIT AND VEG
appointment → BUSINESS, DOCTOR, HAIRDRESSER'S
arm → BODY
armbands → BEACH
arrival → RAILWAY STATION
arrive, to → COACH TRAVEL
ashtray → SMOKING
asparagus → FOOD – FRUIT AND VEG
aspirin → CHEMIST'S
attendant → PETROL STATION, TOILETS
aubergine → FOOD – FRUIT AND VEG
automatic → CAR PARTS
avalanche → WINTER SPORTS
avocado → FOOD – FRUIT AND VEG
avoid, to → ROAD CONDITIONS
baby → CHILDREN
baby food → CHILDREN
baby wipes → TOILETRIES
babysitter → CHILDREN
babysitting service → CHILDREN
back → BODY
bad → DESCRIBING THINGS
bag → LUGGAGE
baggage reclaim → AIRPORT
balcony → ACCOMMODATION
ball → SPORTS
bananas → FOOD – FRUIT AND VEG

bandage → ACCIDENTS – INJURIES, CHEMIST'S
bank → MONEY
baptism → CELEBRATIONS
bar → ENTERTAINMENT, HOTEL DESK
bathroom → ACCOMMODATION
battery → CAR PARTS
beach → BEACH
beautiful → DESCRIBING THINGS
bed → DOCTOR
bedding → SELF-CATERING
bedroom → SELF-CATERING
beef → FOOD – GENERAL
beer → DRINKS
beetroot → FOOD – FRUIT AND VEG
begin, to → NIGHTLIFE
beige → COLOURS AND SHAPES
belt → CLOTHES
bend → DRIVING ABROAD
best wishes → CELEBRATIONS
big → CLOTHES, COLOURS AND SHAPES
bigger → BUYING
bill → EATING OUT, ORDERING, PAYING, ROOM SERVICE
biro → STATIONERY
birthday → CELEBRATIONS
birthday card → STATIONERY
bit, a b. → DENTIST
bitten → DOCTOR
bitter → DESCRIBING THINGS
black → COLOURS AND SHAPES, PHOTOGRAPHY
black coffee → DRINKS
black ice → ROAD CONDITIONS
blanket → ROOM SERVICE

bleeding → ACCIDENTS – INJURIES, DENTIST
blind → PERSONAL DETAILS
blood group → DOCTOR
blood pressure → DOCTOR
blouse → CLOTHES
blow-dry → HAIRDRESSER'S
blue → COLOURS AND SHAPES
blusher → TOILETRIES
boat → BEACH
boat trip → TRIPS AND EXCURSIONS
body → BODY
bone → BODY
bonnet → CAR PARTS
book → STATIONERY
book of tickets → CITY TRAVEL
book, to → ENTERTAINMENT, TRAVEL AGENT
booking → HOTEL DESK, TRAVEL AGENT
booking office → ENTERTAINMENT
boot → CAR PARTS
bottle → CHILDREN, WINES AND SPIRITS
bottle opener → USEFUL ITEMS
bow → SAILING
box of matches → SMOKING
boy → CHILDREN
bra → CLOTHES
bracelet → GIFTS AND SOUVENIRS
brake fluid → CAR PARTS
brakes → CAR PARTS
brand → SMOKING
brandy → WINES AND SPIRITS
bread → EATING OUT, FOOD – GENERAL

breakdown van → BREAKDOWNS
breakfast → ACCOMMODATION
breast → BODY
breathe, to → ACCIDENTS – INJURIES
breeze → WEATHER
bring, to → WINES AND SPIRITS
Britain → CONVERSATION – GENERAL, PERSONAL DETAILS, TELEPHONE
British → CUSTOMS AND PASSPORTS, PROBLEMS
broken → COMPLAINTS, REPAIRS
broken down → BREAKDOWNS
brooch → GIFTS AND SOUVENIRS
broom → USEFUL ITEMS
brown → COLOURS AND SHAPES
bucket → BEACH
buffet → RAILWAY STATION
buffet car → TRAIN TRAVEL
bulb → BREAKDOWNS
bureau de change → MONEY
bus → AIRPORT, CITY TRAVEL, COACH TRAVEL, TRIPS AND EXCURSIONS
bus depot → COACH TRAVEL
bus stop → CITY TRAVEL
bus tour → TRIPS AND EXCURSIONS
business → CUSTOMS AND PASSPORTS, PERSONAL DETAILS
business card → BUSINESS
butter → FOOD – GENERAL
buttocks → BODY
button → CLOTHES, REPAIRS
buy, to → GIFTS AND SOUVENIRS
cabaret → NIGHTLIFE
cabin → FERRIES
cablecar → WINTER SPORTS

café → EATING OUT
call, to → HOTEL DESK
calm → WEATHER
camera → PHOTOGRAPHY
camp, to → CAMPING AND CARAVANNING
camp-bed → CAMPING AND CARAVANNING
campsite → CAMPING AND CARAVANNING
can → PETROL STATION
can opener → USEFUL ITEMS
canoe → WATERSPORTS
captain → FERRIES
car → ACCIDENTS – CARS, AIRPORT, BREAKDOWNS, CAR HIRE
car documents → CAR HIRE
car number → POLICE
car park → DRIVING ABROAD
car wash → PETROL STATION
carafe → WINES AND SPIRITS
caravan → CAMPING AND CARAVANNING
carburettor → CAR PARTS
cardigan → CLOTHES
carrier bag → SHOPPING
carrots → FOOD – FRUIT AND VEG
cartridge → PHOTOGRAPHY
case → LUGGAGE
cash → MONEY, PAYING
cash advance → MONEY
cash desk → PAYING, SHOPPING
cashier → PAYING
casino → NIGHTLIFE
cassette → PHOTOGRAPHY
castle → SIGHTSEEING
catalogue → BUSINESS

catch, to → COACH TRAVEL
cathedral → CHURCH AND WORSHIP, SIGHTSEEING
Catholic → CHURCH AND WORSHIP
cauliflower → FOOD – FRUIT AND VEG
celery → FOOD – FRUIT AND VEG
chains → ROAD CONDITIONS
chair → USEFUL ITEMS
chairlift → WINTER SPORTS
champagne → WINES AND SPIRITS
change → MONEY, PAYING, TAXIS, TELEPHONE
change, to → AIRPORT, BEACH, CITY TRAVEL, RAILWAY STATION, WEATHER
changing room → SHOPPING
Channel, the → FERRIES
chapel → CHURCH AND WORSHIP
charge → PAYING
chauffeur → CAR HIRE
cheap → TRAVEL AGENT
cheaper → BUYING, PAYING
check in, to → AIRPORT, LUGGAGE
check, to → PETROL STATION
check-in desk → AIRPORT
cheek → BODY
cheers! → CELEBRATIONS
cheese → EATING OUT, FOOD – GENERAL
chemist's → ASKING QUESTIONS
cheque → PAYING
cheque book → MONEY
cheque card → PAYING
cherries → FOOD – FRUIT AND VEG

chest → BODY
chicken → FOOD – GENERAL
child → CHILDREN
children → CHILDREN
chilled → WINES AND SPIRITS
chocolates → GIFTS AND SOUVENIRS
choke → CAR PARTS
christening → CELEBRATIONS
Christmas → CELEBRATIONS
church → CHURCH AND WORSHIP
churchyard → CHURCH AND WORSHIP
cigar → SMOKING
cigarette papers → SMOKING
cigarettes → SMOKING
cine-camera → PHOTOGRAPHY
cinema → ENTERTAINMENT
circular → COLOURS AND SHAPES
city → MAPS AND GUIDES
clean → DESCRIBING THINGS
clean, to → CLEANING, PETROL STATION
cleaner → SELF-CATERING
cleansing cream → TOILETRIES
clear → ROAD CONDITIONS
clerk → POST OFFICE
climbing → SPORTS
close → ACCIDENTS – CARS
close, to → SHOPPING, TIME PHRASES
closed → SHOPPING
cloth → USEFUL ITEMS
clothes → CLOTHES
clothespeg → USEFUL ITEMS
clouds → WEATHER
club → ENTERTAINMENT
clutch → CAR PARTS

dark → COLOURS AND SHAPES

date → DATES AND CALENDAR

date of birth → PERSONAL DETAILS

daughter → PERSONAL DETAILS

day → WEATHER

dead → ACCIDENTS – INJURIES

deaf → PERSONAL DETAILS

deck → FERRIES

deck chair → BEACH

declare, to → CUSTOMS AND PASSPORTS

deep → BEACH

denim → CLOTHES

dentist → DENTIST

dentures → DENTIST

deodorant → TOILETRIES

department → BUYING

department store → BUYING

departure → RAILWAY STATION

deposit → PAYING

desk → HOTEL DESK

dessert → EATING OUT

details → BUSINESS

detour → ROAD CONDITIONS

develop, to → PHOTOGRAPHY

diabetic → DOCTOR

dialling code → TELEPHONE

dialling tone → TELEPHONE

diarrhoea → CHEMIST'S, DOCTOR

dictionary → MAPS AND GUIDES

diesel → PETROL STATION

difficult → DESCRIBING THINGS

dinghy → SAILING

dinner → HOTEL DESK

directory → TELEPHONE

dirty → COMPLAINTS, DESCRIBING THINGS

disabled → ACCOMMODATION

disco → NIGHTLIFE

discount → PAYING

dish → ORDERING, USEFUL ITEMS

disinfectant → CLEANING

dislocate, to → ACCIDENTS – INJURIES

disposable nappies → CHILDREN

distilled water → PETROL STATION

distributor → CAR PARTS

dizzy → DOCTOR

doctor → DOCTOR, EMERGENCIES

documents → ACCIDENTS – CARS, POLICE

dollars → MONEY

door → SELF-CATERING

double bed → ACCOMMODATION

double room → ACCOMMODATION

dozen → MEASUREMENTS

draught → DRINKS

drawing book → STATIONERY

dreadful → WEATHER

dress → CLOTHES

drink → EATING OUT

drinking chocolate → DRINKS

drinking water → CAMPING AND CARAVANNING, DRINKS

drive, to → CAR HIRE

driver → CITY TRAVEL, COACH TRAVEL, TRAIN TRAVEL

driving licence → ACCIDENTS – CARS, DRIVING ABROAD

dry → WINES AND SPIRITS

dry cleaner's → CLEANING

dry, to → CLEANING

dummy → CHILDREN

duty-free → FERRIES

film show → COACH TRAVEL
filter → SMOKING
filter-tipped → SMOKING
fine → GREETINGS, POLICE, WEATHER
finger → BODY
fire → EMERGENCIES
fire brigade → EMERGENCIES
first class → RAILWAY STATION
fish → FOOD – GENERAL
fish, to → WATERSPORTS
fishing → SPORTS
flash → PHOTOGRAPHY
flash bulb → PHOTOGRAPHY
flash cube → PHOTOGRAPHY
flask → USEFUL ITEMS
flat tyre → BREAKDOWNS
flaw → COMPLAINTS
flight → AIRPORT
flight bag → LUGGAGE
flippers → WATERSPORTS
flour → FOOD – GENERAL
flowers → GIFTS AND SOUVENIRS
flush, to → TOILETS
fly sheet → CAMPING AND CARAVANNING
fly, to → TRAVEL AGENT
fog → ROAD CONDITIONS, WEATHER
foggy → WEATHER
food → SHOPPING
food poisoning → DOCTOR
foot → BODY
forget, to → EMERGENCIES
forgotten → PROBLEMS
fork → USEFUL ITEMS
form → POST OFFICE
franc → MONEY

France → CONVERSATION – GENERAL
free → TRAIN TRAVEL
French → CONVERSATION – MEETING
french beans → FOOD – FRUIT AND VEG
frequent → CITY TRAVEL
fridge → SELF-CATERING
fringe → HAIRDRESSER'S
frost → ROAD CONDITIONS, WEATHER
fruit juice → DRINKS
frying-pan → USEFUL ITEMS
full board → ACCOMMODATION
fun fair → ENTERTAINMENT
fur → CLOTHES
fuse → CAR PARTS, SELF-CATERING
garage → BREAKDOWNS, PETROL STATION
garlic → FOOD – FRUIT AND VEG
gas → SELF-CATERING
gas cylinder → CAMPING AND CARAVANNING
gas refill → SMOKING
gears → CAR PARTS
get in, to → NIGHTLIFE, SIGHTSEEING
get off, to → CITY TRAVEL, COACH TRAVEL
get through, to → TELEPHONE
gift → SHOPPING
gift shop → GIFTS AND SOUVENIRS
gin → WINES AND SPIRITS
girl → CHILDREN
Giro account → POST OFFICE

glass → DRINKS, WINES AND SPIRITS
glasses → USEFUL ITEMS
gloves → CLOTHES
glue → REPAIRS
goggles → WATERSPORTS
gold → COLOURS AND SHAPES
golf → SPORTS
good → ASKING QUESTIONS, DESCRIBING THINGS
good afternoon → GREETINGS
good evening → GREETINGS
good morning → GREETINGS
good night → GREETINGS
goodbye → GREETINGS
gown → HAIRDRESSER'S
gramme → BUYING, MEASUREMENTS
grapefruit → FOOD – FRUIT AND VEG
grapes → FOOD – FRUIT AND VEG
green → COLOURS AND SHAPES
green card → ACCIDENTS – CARS, POLICE
grey → COLOURS AND SHAPES
group → TRIPS AND EXCURSIONS
guard → RAILWAY STATION, TRAIN TRAVEL
guide book → MAPS AND GUIDES, SIGHTSEEING
guided tour → SIGHTSEEING, TRIPS AND EXCURSIONS
gums → DENTIST
guy rope → CAMPING AND CARAVANNING
gym shoes → SPORTS
gymnasium → SPORTS
hair → HAIRDRESSER'S
hair spray → HAIRDRESSER'S

hairbrush → USEFUL ITEMS
hairdryer → ROOM SERVICE
hairgrip → USEFUL ITEMS
half bottle → WINES AND SPIRITS
half fare → CITY TRAVEL
half-board → ACCOMMODATION
ham → FOOD – GENERAL
hammer → REPAIRS
hand → BODY
hand cream → TOILETRIES
hand luggage → LUGGAGE
hand-made → GIFTS AND SOUVENIRS
handbag → EMERGENCIES
handbrake → CAR PARTS
handkerchief → USEFUL ITEMS
handle → REPAIRS
harbour → SAILING
hard → DESCRIBING THINGS
hat → CLOTHES
hay fever → DOCTOR
hazard lights → BREAKDOWNS
head → BODY
headache → CHEMIST'S, DOCTOR
headlights → CAR PARTS
heart → BODY
heater → SELF-CATERING
heating → SELF-CATERING
heavy → DESCRIBING THINGS, LUGGAGE
hello → GREETINGS
help → EMERGENCIES
help, to → ASKING QUESTIONS, PROBLEMS
high chair → CHILDREN
high tide → BEACH
hill-walking → SPORTS

hire, to → AIRPORT, CAR HIRE, ENTERTAINMENT
hold, to → TELEPHONE
hold-up → ROAD CONDITIONS
hole → COMPLAINTS
holiday → CELEBRATIONS, CONVERSATION – GENERAL
horrible → DESCRIBING THINGS
hose → CAR PARTS, PETROL STATION
hospital → ACCIDENTS – INJURIES, EMERGENCIES
hot → DESCRIBING THINGS, WEATHER
hotel → TAXIS, TRAVEL AGENT
hour → TIME PHRASES
house wine → WINES AND SPIRITS
hovercraft → FERRIES
hurry → TAXIS
hurt, to → ACCIDENTS – INJURIES, DENTIST
husband → PERSONAL DETAILS
ice → DRINKS
ice cream → SIGHTSEEING
icy → WINTER SPORTS
ignition → CAR PARTS
ill → DOCTOR
included → ORDERING, PAYING
indicator → CAR PARTS
inflamed → DOCTOR
information office → DIRECTIONS
injection → DENTIST, DOCTOR
injured → ACCIDENTS – INJURIES
ink → STATIONERY
ink cartridge → STATIONERY
insect bite → CHEMIST'S
insect repellant → CHEMIST'S

instructor → WINTER SPORTS
insurance certificate → ACCIDENTS – CARS, POLICE
insurance company → ACCIDENTS – CARS
insurance cover → CAR HIRE
interesting → DESCRIBING THINGS
international → POST OFFICE
Irish → PERSONAL DETAILS
iron → ROOM SERVICE
iron, to → CLEANING
jack → BREAKDOWNS
jacket → CLOTHES
jam → FOOD – GENERAL
jam, to → PHOTOGRAPHY
jazz → ENTERTAINMENT
jeans → CLOTHES
joint → BODY
joint passport → CUSTOMS AND PASSPORTS
jump leads → BREAKDOWNS
keep, to → TAXIS
key → HOTEL DESK
kidney → BODY
kidneys → FOOD – GENERAL
kilo → BUYING, FOOD – GENERAL, MEASUREMENTS, SHOPPING
kilometre → ASKING QUESTIONS
kitchen → SELF-CATERING
knee → BODY
knife → USEFUL ITEMS
lace → CLOTHES
lake → TRIPS AND EXCURSIONS
lamb → FOOD – GENERAL
land, to → AIRPORT
large → CAR HIRE
last, to → NIGHTLIFE

late → TIME PHRASES
later → TELEPHONE
launderette → CLEANING
laundry service → CLEANING
lavatory → PETROL STATION
lawyer → ACCIDENTS – CARS,
  POLICE
laxative → CHEMIST'S
layered → HAIRDRESSER'S
leak → BREAKDOWNS
leather → CLOTHES
leave, to → COACH TRAVEL,
  TIME PHRASES
leeks → FOOD – FRUIT AND VEG
left → DIRECTIONS
left luggage → LUGGAGE,
  RAILWAY STATION
leg → BODY
lemon → COLOURS AND SHAPES,
  FOOD – FRUIT AND VEG
lemon tea → DRINKS
lemonade → DRINKS
lens → PHOTOGRAPHY
lens cover → PHOTOGRAPHY
less → MEASUREMENTS
lessons → SPORTS
let off, to → COACH TRAVEL
letter → POST OFFICE
lettuce → FOOD – FRUIT AND
  VEG
life jacket → FERRIES,
  WATERSPORTS
lifeboat → FERRIES
lifeguard → BEACH
lift → ACCOMMODATION
light → CLOTHES, COLOURS AND
  SHAPES, DESCRIBING THINGS,
  SELF-CATERING, SMOKING
lighter → SMOKING

like, to → CONVERSATION –
  GENERAL
line → TELEPHONE
lipstick → TOILETRIES
liqueur → WINES AND SPIRITS
literature → BUSINESS
litre → FOOD – GENERAL,
  MEASUREMENTS, PETROL
  STATION
live, to → PERSONAL DETAILS
liver → BODY, FOOD – GENERAL
living room → SELF-CATERING
local → MAPS AND GUIDES,
  ORDERING
lock → COMPLAINTS
locked out → ROOM SERVICE
locker → LUGGAGE
long → COLOURS AND SHAPES,
  DESCRIBING THINGS,
  HAIRDRESSER'S
look for, to → SHOPPING
loose → REPAIRS
lost → PROBLEMS
lost property office
  → EMERGENCIES
lounge → AIRPORT, HOTEL DESK
lovely → DESCRIBING THINGS,
  WEATHER
low tide → BEACH
luggage → LUGGAGE
luggage allowance → LUGGAGE
luggage hold → COACH TRAVEL
luggage rack → COACH TRAVEL,
  LUGGAGE
luggage tag → STATIONERY
luggage trolley → LUGGAGE
lunch → ACCOMMODATION
lung → BODY
magazine → STATIONERY

main → SHOPPING
main course → EATING OUT
major road → DRIVING ABROAD
mallet → CAMPING AND
  CARAVANNING
manager → HOTEL DESK
map → MAPS AND GUIDES
margarine → FOOD – GENERAL
market → SHOPPING
Martini → WINES AND SPIRITS
mascara → TOILETRIES
mass → CHURCH AND WORSHIP
mast → SAILING
matches → SMOKING
material → CLOTHES
mauve → COLOURS AND SHAPES
meal → ORDERING
measure, to → CLOTHES
mechanic → BREAKDOWNS
medicine → DOCTOR
medium → WINES AND SPIRITS
medium rare → MEASUREMENTS
melon → FOOD – FRUIT AND VEG
member → NIGHTLIFE
menu → EATING OUT, ORDERING
message → BUSINESS
meter → SELF-CATERING, TAXIS
metre → SHOPPING
mild → WEATHER
milk → DRINKS, FOOD –
  GENERAL
mince → FOOD – GENERAL
mind, to → SMOKING
mineral water → DRINKS
minister → CHURCH AND
  WORSHIP
minor road → DRIVING ABROAD
minute → TIME
mirror → TOILETS

missing → EMERGENCIES
mist → WEATHER
misty → WEATHER
moisturizer → TOILETRIES
money → MONEY
money order → POST OFFICE
more → MEASUREMENTS
morning → TIME PHRASES
mosque → CHURCH AND
  WORSHIP
mother → TOILETS
motor boat → WATERSPORTS
motorway → DRIVING ABROAD
mouth → BODY
move, to → ACCIDENTS –
  INJURIES
movie camera → PHOTOGRAPHY
municipal → WATERSPORTS
muscle → BODY
museum → SIGHTSEEING
mushrooms → FOOD – FRUIT
  AND VEG
mustard → FOOD – GENERAL
nail → REPAIRS
nail file → TOILETRIES
nail polish → TOILETRIES
nail polish remover
  → TOILETRIES
name → PERSONAL DETAILS
nappy → CHILDREN
national → CUSTOMS AND
  PASSPORTS
nearest → DIRECTIONS
neck → BODY
necklace → GIFTS AND
  SOUVENIRS
need, to → DOCTOR
needle and thread → USEFUL
  ITEMS

negative → PHOTOGRAPHY
new → DESCRIBING THINGS
New Year → CELEBRATIONS
newspaper → STATIONERY
next → FERRIES, RAILWAY
STATION
nice → WEATHER
night → HOTEL DESK
night club → NIGHTLIFE
nightdress → CLOTHES
no → CONVERSATION – MEETING
noisy → COMPLAINTS
non-smoking → AIRPORT,
RAILWAY STATION
nose → BODY
note → MONEY
note pad → STATIONERY
number → PERSONAL DETAILS
nylon → CLOTHES
oar → WATERSPORTS
oblong → COLOURS AND SHAPES
offence → ACCIDENTS – CARS
office → PERSONAL DETAILS
oil → FOOD – GENERAL, PETROL
STATION
old → DESCRIBING THINGS
olives → FOOD – FRUIT AND VEG
one-way → DRIVING ABROAD
onions → FOOD – FRUIT AND
VEG
open → SHOPPING
open, to → SIGHTSEEING, TIME
PHRASES
operate, to → CAR HIRE
operation → DOCTOR
operator → TELEPHONE
orange → COLOURS AND SHAPES
oranges → FOOD – FRUIT AND
VEG

orchestra → ENTERTAINMENT
order → ORDERING
organized → TRIPS AND
EXCURSIONS
ornament → GIFTS AND
SOUVENIRS
outside line → ROOM SERVICE
oval → COLOURS AND SHAPES
over → DIRECTIONS
over there → DIRECTIONS
overheat, to → BREAKDOWNS
packet → SMOKING
paddling pool → WATERSPORTS
pain → DOCTOR
painful → DOCTOR
painting book → STATIONERY
paints → STATIONERY
pants → CLOTHES
paper → STATIONERY
paper bag → SHOPPING
paperback → STATIONERY
paperclip → STATIONERY
parcel → POST OFFICE
park → SIGHTSEEING
park, to → DRIVING ABROAD
parking disk → DRIVING
ABROAD
parking meter → DRIVING
ABROAD
parking ticket → DRIVING
ABROAD
parting → HAIRDRESSER'S
parts → BREAKDOWNS
party → TRIPS AND EXCURSIONS
pass → ROAD CONDITIONS
passport → EMERGENCIES,
PERSONAL DETAILS
passport control → AIRPORT
pay, to → PAYING

payment → PAYING
peaches → FOOD – FRUIT AND VEG
pears → FOOD – FRUIT AND VEG
peas → FOOD – FRUIT AND VEG
pen → STATIONERY
pencil → STATIONERY
pencil sharpener → STATIONERY
penicillin → DOCTOR
penknife → USEFUL ITEMS
pepper → FOOD – FRUIT AND VEG, FOOD – GENERAL
per → CAMPING AND CARAVANNING
performance → NIGHTLIFE
perfume → TOILETRIES
perm → HAIRDRESSER'S
petrol → BREAKDOWNS, PETROL STATION
petrol pump → PETROL STATION
petrol station → PETROL STATION
petrol tank → BREAKDOWNS
petticoat → CLOTHES
phone → TELEPHONE
phone box → TELEPHONE
phone call → TELEPHONE
phone, to → TELEPHONE
photocopy, to → BUSINESS
photos → PHOTOGRAPHY
phrase book → MAPS AND GUIDES
picnic → HOTEL DESK
pill → DOCTOR
pin → REPAIRS
pineapple → FOOD – FRUIT AND VEG
pink → COLOURS AND SHAPES
pint → MEASUREMENTS

pipe → SMOKING
pipe cleaners → SMOKING
pipe tobacco → SMOKING
plane → AIRPORT
plate → USEFUL ITEMS
platform → RAILWAY STATION
play → ENTERTAINMENT
play, to → ENTERTAINMENT, SPORTS
playroom → CHILDREN
pleasant → DESCRIBING THINGS
plug → USEFUL ITEMS
plums → FOOD – FRUIT AND VEG
pointed → COLOURS AND SHAPES
points → CAR PARTS
poisoning → DOCTOR
police → ACCIDENTS – CARS, POLICE
police car → POLICE
police station → EMERGENCIES, POLICE
policeman → POLICE
polyester → CLOTHES
pony-trekking → SPORTS
pork → FOOD – GENERAL
port → WINES AND SPIRITS
porter → HOTEL DESK, LUGGAGE
portion → MEASUREMENTS
possible → SPORTS
post office → POST OFFICE
postage → POST OFFICE
postcard → STATIONERY
pot → DRINKS
potatoes → FOOD – FRUIT AND VEG
pottery → GIFTS AND SOUVENIRS
pound → FOOD – GENERAL, MEASUREMENTS
pounds → MONEY

pram → CHILDREN
prefer, to → BUYING
pregnant → DOCTOR
prescription → CHEMIST'S
present → GIFTS AND SOUVENIRS
priest → CHURCH AND WORSHIP
prints → PHOTOGRAPHY
private → BEACH
propeller → SAILING
Protestant → CHURCH AND WORSHIP
public → SIGHTSEEING
public holiday → CELEBRATIONS
purple → COLOURS AND SHAPES
purse → MONEY
purser → FERRIES
push chair → CHILDREN
put through, to → TELEPHONE
put, to → ROOM SERVICE
pyjamas → CLOTHES
quarter → MEASUREMENTS
quickly → EMERGENCIES
quiet → BEACH
rabbi → CHURCH AND WORSHIP
racket → SPORTS
radiator → CAR PARTS
radio → CAR HIRE
radishes → FOOD – FRUIT AND VEG
rain, to → WEATHER
raincoat → CLOTHES
rare → ORDERING
raspberries → FOOD – FRUIT AND VEG
rate → MONEY
razor → TOILETRIES
razor blades → TOILETRIES
ready → ASKING QUESTIONS
receipt → PAYING

receiver → TELEPHONE
reclining seat → FERRIES
recommend, to → ORDERING
red → COLOURS AND SHAPES, WINES AND SPIRITS
reduction → PAYING
reel → PHOTOGRAPHY
refill → STATIONERY
registered → POST OFFICE
regulations → POLICE
reheel, to → REPAIRS
remove, to → CLEANING
rent, to → SPORTS
rental → SELF-CATERING
repair → BREAKDOWNS
repair, to → REPAIRS
repeat, to → PROBLEMS
reply coupon → POST OFFICE
reservation → HOTEL DESK, RAILWAY STATION
reserve, to → HOTEL DESK, RAILWAY STATION
restaurant → EATING OUT
restaurant car → TRAIN TRAVEL
return → RAILWAY STATION
return ticket → FERRIES
reversing lights → CAR PARTS
rice → FOOD – GENERAL
riding → SPORTS
right → DIRECTIONS
ring → GIFTS AND SOUVENIRS
rink → WINTER SPORTS
river → WATERSPORTS
road → DRIVING ABROAD
road conditions → ROAD CONDITIONS
road map → MAPS AND GUIDES
road sign → DIRECTIONS
road works → ROAD CONDITIONS

rob, to → POLICE
room → HOTEL DESK
room service → HOTEL DESK
rope → USEFUL ITEMS
rosé → WINES AND SPIRITS
rough → DESCRIBING THINGS,
  FERRIES
round → COLOURS AND SHAPES
route → ROAD CONDITIONS
rowing boat → WATERSPORTS
rubber → STATIONERY
rudder → SAILING
run out, to → BREAKDOWNS,
  PROBLEMS
safe → BEACH, CHEMIST'S
safety pin → REPAIRS, USEFUL
  ITEMS
sail → SAILING
sailboard → WATERSPORTS
sailing → FERRIES
salt → FOOD – GENERAL
sample → BUSINESS
sandals → CLOTHES
sandwich → EATING OUT
sanitary towels → CHEMIST'S
saucepan → USEFUL ITEMS
scarf → CLOTHES
scissors → USEFUL ITEMS
Scotch → WINES AND SPIRITS
Scottish → PERSONAL DETAILS
screw → REPAIRS
screwdriver → REPAIRS
scuba-diving → WATERSPORTS
sea → BEACH, FERRIES
seasick → SAILING
season ticket → CITY TRAVEL
seat → COACH TRAVEL, RAILWAY
  STATION, TOILETS, TRAIN
  TRAVEL

seat belt → DRIVING ABROAD
second class → RAILWAY
  STATION, TRAVEL AGENT
secretary → BUSINESS
see, to → SIGHTSEEING
sell, to → BUYING
send, to → POST OFFICE
senior citizen → TRIPS AND
  EXCURSIONS
serious → ACCIDENTS – INJURIES
serve, to → ORDERING
served, to be → COMPLAINTS
service → CHURCH AND
  WORSHIP, ORDERING
set → HAIRDRESSER'S
set menu → EATING OUT
shade → COLOURS AND SHAPES
shampoo → TOILETRIES
shandy → DRINKS
shattered → BREAKDOWNS
shaving cream → TOILETRIES
sheet → SELF-CATERING
sherry → WINES AND SPIRITS
shiny → COLOURS AND SHAPES
ship → FERRIES
shirt → CLOTHES
shock absorber → CAR PARTS
shoes → CLOTHES
shop → BUYING
shopping area → SHOPPING
shopping bag → SHOPPING
short → DESCRIBING THINGS,
  HAIRDRESSER'S
short-cut → DRIVING ABROAD
shorts → CLOTHES, SPORTS
shoulder → BODY
show → NIGHTLIFE
show, to → DIRECTIONS, MAPS
  AND GUIDES

shower → SELF-CATERING
shutter → PHOTOGRAPHY
sick → DOCTOR, TRIPS AND
  EXCURSIONS
sign → DRIVING ABROAD
signature → PAYING
silk → CLOTHES
silver → COLOURS AND SHAPES
single → RAILWAY STATION
single bed → ACCOMMODATION
single room
  → ACCOMMODATION
sink → CLEANING
sit, to → CONVERSATION –
  MEETING
site → CAMPING AND
  CARAVANNING
skates → WINTER SPORTS
skating → WINTER SPORTS
ski boot → WINTER SPORTS
ski pole → WINTER SPORTS
skin → BODY
skirt → CLOTHES
skis → WINTER SPORTS
sleep, to → DOCTOR
sleeper → RAILWAY STATION
sleeping bag → CAMPING AND
  CARAVANNING
sleeping car → TRAIN TRAVEL
slice → MEASUREMENTS
slides → PHOTOGRAPHY
slip, to → ACCIDENTS – INJURIES
slow → DESCRIBING THINGS
small → COLOURS AND SHAPES
smaller → BUYING
smoke, to → SMOKING
smooth → DESCRIBING THINGS,
  FERRIES
snack bar → AIRPORT

snorkel → WATERSPORTS
snow → WINTER SPORTS
snow, to → WEATHER
snowed up → ROAD CONDITIONS
soap → TOILETRIES
socket → ROOM SERVICE
socks → CLOTHES
soft → DESCRIBING THINGS
soft drink → DRINKS
son → PERSONAL DETAILS
sore → CHEMIST'S, DENTIST,
  DOCTOR
sorry → CONVERSATION –
  GENERAL
soup → EATING OUT, FOOD –
  GENERAL
sour → DESCRIBING THINGS
souvenir → GIFTS AND
  SOUVENIRS
spade → BEACH
spanner → BREAKDOWNS
spark plugs → CAR PARTS
sparkling → WINES AND SPIRITS
speak, to → CONVERSATION –
  MEETING, PROBLEMS,
  TELEPHONE
special → TRAVEL AGENT
special rate → CHILDREN
speciality → ORDERING
spicy → DESCRIBING THINGS
spinach → FOOD – FRUIT AND
  VEG
spirits → CUSTOMS AND
  PASSPORTS
sponge → TOILETRIES
sponge bag → TOILETRIES
spoon → USEFUL ITEMS
sports → SPORTS

sprain, to → ACCIDENTS – INJURIES
square → COLOURS AND SHAPES
squash → SPORTS
stain → CLEANING
stall → SHOPPING
stamps → POST OFFICE
stapler → STATIONERY
staples → STATIONERY
starter → EATING OUT
station → TAXIS
stay → HOTEL DESK
stay, to → CUSTOMS AND PASSPORTS, DOCTOR
steak → FOOD – GENERAL
steering → CAR PARTS
steering wheel → CAR PARTS
sterling → MONEY
stern → SAILING
sticking plaster → CHEMIST'S
stitching → REPAIRS
stockings → CLOTHES
stolen → EMERGENCIES
stomach → BODY
stomach upset → DOCTOR
stop, to → TAXIS, TRAIN TRAVEL, TRIPS AND EXCURSIONS
stopping train → TRAIN TRAVEL
straight → HAIRDRESSER'S
straight on → DIRECTIONS
strawberries → FOOD – FRUIT AND VEG
streaks → HAIRDRESSER'S
street map → MAPS AND GUIDES
street plan → SIGHTSEEING
string → REPAIRS
strong → DESCRIBING THINGS
student → PERSONAL DETAILS

stung → ACCIDENTS – INJURIES
styling mousse → HAIRDRESSER'S
suede → CLOTHES
sugar → FOOD – GENERAL
suit (man's) → CLOTHES
suit (woman's) → CLOTHES
suitable → SHOPPING
suitcase → LUGGAGE
sun-tan cream → TOILETRIES
sunburn → ACCIDENTS – INJURIES
sunglasses → BEACH
sunny → WEATHER
sunshade → BEACH
sunstroke → ACCIDENTS – INJURIES
suntan oil → BEACH
supermarket → BUYING
supplement → RAILWAY STATION
swallow, to → DOCTOR
sweater → CLOTHES
sweet → DESCRIBING THINGS, WINES AND SPIRITS
swim, to → BEACH
swimming → SPORTS
swimming pool → SPORTS
swimsuit → BEACH, CLOTHES
synagogue → CHURCH AND WORSHIP
t-shirt → CLOTHES
table → EATING OUT, ORDERING
table linen → GIFTS AND SOUVENIRS
tablet → DOCTOR
tailback → ROAD CONDITIONS
take out, to → DENTIST
take up, to → HOTEL DESK

take, to → CHEMIST'S, DIRECTIONS, SPORTS
talc → TOILETRIES
tampons → CHEMIST'S
tap → CLEANING
tape → REPAIRS
tax → PAYING
taxi → TAXIS
tea → DRINKS, FOOD – GENERAL
telegram → POST OFFICE
telephone → PETROL STATION
telex → BUSINESS
tell, to → TRAIN TRAVEL
temperature → DOCTOR, WEATHER
temporary → REPAIRS
tennis → SPORTS
tent → CAMPING AND CARAVANNING
tent peg → CAMPING AND CARAVANNING
tent pole → CAMPING AND CARAVANNING
terrace → EATING OUT
thank you → CONVERSATION – MEETING
that one → ORDERING
theatre → ENTERTAINMENT
thick → COLOURS AND SHAPES
thin → COLOURS AND SHAPES
third → MEASUREMENTS
this one → ORDERING
throat → BODY
through → DIRECTIONS
thumb → BODY
thunderstorm → WEATHER
ticket → CITY TRAVEL, ENTERTAINMENT, TRIPS AND EXCURSIONS

ticket collector → TRAIN TRAVEL
ticket office → RAILWAY STATION
tie → CLOTHES
tights → CLOTHES
till → PAYING
time → TIME, TIME PHRASES
timetable board → RAILWAY STATION
tin → FOOD – GENERAL
tip, to → TIPPING
tissues → CHEMIST'S, TOILETRIES
tobacco → CUSTOMS AND PASSPORTS
toe → BODY
toilet → TOILETS
toilet paper → TOILETS
toilet water → TOILETRIES
toll → DRIVING ABROAD
tomatoes → FOOD – FRUIT AND VEG
tomorrow → BUSINESS
tongue → BODY
tonight → NIGHTLIFE
too → CLOTHES
tooth → DENTIST
toothache → DENTIST
toothbrush → TOILETRIES
toothpaste → TOILETRIES
torch → USEFUL ITEMS
torn → REPAIRS
tour → TRIPS AND EXCURSIONS
tourist → DIRECTIONS
tourist office → MAPS AND GUIDES
tourist ticket → CITY TRAVEL
tow, to → BREAKDOWNS
towel → BEACH, HAIRDRESSER'S

town → CITY TRAVEL
town centre → CITY TRAVEL
town plan → MAPS AND GUIDES
trade fair → BUSINESS
traffic → ROAD CONDITIONS
traffic jam → ROAD CONDITIONS
traffic lights → DRIVING
  ABROAD
traffic offence → POLICE
traffic warden → POLICE
trailer → CAMPING AND
  CARAVANNING
train → CITY TRAVEL, TRAIN
  TRAVEL
transfer charge call
  → TELEPHONE
transfer, to → MONEY
transit, in t. → LUGGAGE
travel, to → GIFTS AND
  SOUVENIRS
traveller's cheques → MONEY
trim, to → HAIRDRESSER'S
trip → SIGHTSEEING
tripod → PHOTOGRAPHY
trouble → PROBLEMS
trousers → CLOTHES
trunk → LUGGAGE
trunks → CLOTHES
try on, to → CLOTHES
tunnel → ROAD CONDITIONS
turn off, to → COMPLAINTS
turn on, to → COMPLAINTS
turn, to → TAXIS
turning → DIRECTIONS
turquoise → COLOURS AND
  SHAPES
TV lounge → HOTEL DESK
twice → MEASUREMENTS
tyre → CAR PARTS

tyre pressure → PETROL
  STATION
umbrella → USEFUL ITEMS
unconscious → DOCTOR
under → DIRECTIONS
underground station → CITY
  TRAVEL
underground → CITY TRAVEL
understand, to → ASKING
  QUESTIONS
unpleasant → DESCRIBING
  THINGS
upset → CHEMIST'S
urgently → DENTIST
vacancies → CAMPING AND
  CARAVANNING
vacuum cleaner → USEFUL
  ITEMS
veal → FOOD − GENERAL
vegetables → EATING OUT
vending machine → TOILETS
vermouth → WINES AND SPIRITS
vest → CLOTHES
view → SIGHTSEEING
vinegar → FOOD − GENERAL
visit → TRIPS AND EXCURSIONS
vodka → WINES AND SPIRITS
voltage → ROOM SERVICE
wait, to → COMPLAINTS, TAXIS
waiter → ORDERING
waiting room → RAILWAY
  STATION
waitress → ORDERING
walk, to → DIRECTIONS
wallet → MONEY
warm → DESCRIBING THINGS,
  WEATHER
warning triangle
  → BREAKDOWNS

wash, to → CLEANING
washbasin → CLEANING, TOILETS
washing → CLEANING
washing powder → CLEANING
washing-up liquid → USEFUL ITEMS
washroom → CAMPING AND CARAVANNING
waste bin → TOILETS
watch → GIFTS AND SOUVENIRS
water → BEACH, EATING OUT, PETROL STATION
water heater → SELF-CATERING
water-skiing → WATERSPORTS
way → DIRECTIONS
weak → DESCRIBING THINGS
weather → WEATHER
weather forecast → SAILING
wedding → CELEBRATIONS
week → CUSTOMS AND PASSPORTS
well done → ORDERING
Welsh → PERSONAL DETAILS
wet → WEATHER
wetsuit → WATERSPORTS
wheel → CAR PARTS
wheel brace → BREAKDOWNS
white → COLOURS AND SHAPES, WINES AND SPIRITS
white coffee → DRINKS
wife → PERSONAL DETAILS
wind → SAILING
wind-surfing → WATERSPORTS
window → SHOPPING, TRAIN TRAVEL
window seat → AIRPORT
windscreen → CAR PARTS

windscreen washer → CAR PARTS
windscreen wiper → CAR PARTS
windy → WEATHER
wine → WINES AND SPIRITS
wine list → WINES AND SPIRITS
wool → CLOTHES
work, to → COMPLAINTS
wrap, to → BUYING
wrist → BODY
writing paper → STATIONERY
wrong → PAYING
wrong number → TELEPHONE
yellow → COLOURS AND SHAPES
yes → CONVERSATION – MEETING
yoghurt → FOOD – GENERAL
youth hostel → ACCOMMODATION
zip → CLOTHES
zoo → TRIPS AND EXCURSIONS